the sacred art of
FASTING

Other Books in the Preparing to Practice Series

The Sacred Art of Bowing: Preparing to Practice
by Andi Young

The Sacred Art of Chant: Preparing to Practice
by Ana Hernández

the sacred art of
FASTING

preparing
to practice

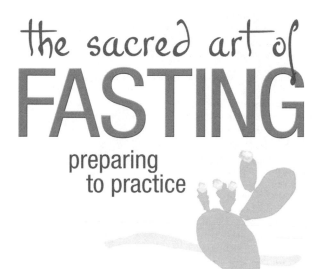

Thomas Ryan, CSP

Walking Together, Finding the Way
SKYLIGHT PATHS® Publishing
Woodstock, Vermont

The Sacred Art of Fasting:
Preparing to Practice

2005 First Printing
© 2005 by Thomas Ryan

For information regarding permission to reprint material from this book, please write or fax your request to SkyLight Paths Publishing, Permissions Department, at the address / fax number listed below, or e-mail your request to permissions@skylightpaths.com.

Library of Congress Cataloging-in-Publication Data
Ryan, Thomas, Father.
The sacred art of fasting / Thomas Ryan.
    p. cm.—(Preparing to practice)
Includes bibliographical references (p.   ).
ISBN 1-59473-078-4 (pbk.)
1. Fasts and feasts. 2. Fasting—Religious aspects. I. Title. II. Series.
BL590.R93 2005
204'.47—dc22

                                                                2004029665

Grateful acknowledgment is given for permission to reprint material from the following sources: Aliza Bulow, "Connecting through Fasting" and Sheryl Condie Kempton, "Fasting: A Gift of Joy."

10 9 8 7 6 5 4 3 2 1
Manufactured in the United States of America
Cover Design: Sara Dismukes

SkyLight Paths Publishing is creating a place where people of different spiritual traditions come together for challenge and inspiration, a place where we can help each other understand the mystery that lies at the heart of our existence.

SkyLight Paths sees both believers and seekers as a community that increasingly transcends traditional boundaries of religion and denomination—people wanting to learn from each other, *walking together, finding the way.*

SkyLight Paths, "Walking Together, Finding the Way," and colophon are trademarks of LongHill Partners, Inc., registered in the U.S. Patent and Trademark Office.

Walking Together, Finding the Way
Published by SkyLight Paths Publishing
A Division of LongHill Partners, Inc.
Sunset Farm Offices, Route 4, P.O. Box 237
Woodstock, VT 05091
Tel: (802) 457-4000   Fax: (802) 457-4004
www.skylightpaths.com

To my parents,
Francis and Genevieve Ryan,
who cultivated in me an appetite for God

CONTENTS

INTRODUCTION

This book is about doing something deeply human—fasting—and the reasons people from almost every religious tradition in the world do it.

Fasting, abstention from food and often drink for a designated period of time, has been practiced for centuries in connection with religious observance. The religions that practice fasting encompass the vast majority of people on the planet: Baha'is, Buddhists, Christians, Confucianists, Hindus, Jains, Jews, Muslims, Native North Americans, and Taoists. You might justifiably conclude that any spiritual practice embraced so universally has to have something going for it. But what, exactly?

In today's secular society, more people than you might guess engage in rational fasting—so called because it is understood to foster health through the purification of the body. Fasting is considered a very rational thing to do, a kind of body-ecology, one of the ways that we exercise care and respect for ourselves.

Normally, the body is constantly working to digest foods, eliminate wastes, fight diseases, replenish worn-out cells, and nourish the blood. Of these, masticating and digesting food is its biggest chore. When there is no food to digest, our energy is turned with fuller force upon the other "projects." Giving our bodies a chance to eliminate the toxic wastes that have been stored in the tissues or held in the pockets of the intestines and that interfere with the proper digestive and blood-building functions is an act of care for

INTRODUCTION

ourselves. As its practitioners know, fasting also calms us and sharpens the senses, helps us think more clearly and sleep better.

When you look at fasting in the different religious traditions of the world, a wider field of values emerges. Not only physical and mental purification are there, but other values, too, such as self-restraint, social solidarity, penance, attunement to God. And it doesn't take long to see that certain values underlying the practice emerge as commonly acknowledged and shared.

The focus of this book is not just upon fasting as a rational act but as a *religious* act. One of its primary objectives is to contribute to a renewed appreciation of fasting as an act of the human spirit in relation to an Other and to your neighbor for whose well-being you recognize a responsibility.

The values at play are of particular interest because the reason you do something changes the nature of the act from within. As each of us developed our moral sense through the interactions of home, friends, and school, we learned that the "why" of what we did made a big difference in how that act was responded to. Why did you wake your little brother? Did you think the house was on fire or were you mad at him? Why does she get to do that and you don't? Is there some special reason or is she just the teacher's favorite? Why are you taking that job? Is it because you like the work or because you can't find anything else? Why did you fire the gun? Was it in self-defense or because you came home upset that night? The *why* that lies behind our behavior is directly linked to what's in our head and heart, and since the two of those working in harmony are what give meaning to our actions, *why* we do something deserves careful attention.

Chapter 1 relates how I personally came to be interested in the subject, and my search for an approach to the practice that took into account not just my body, but my spirit and soul as well. Chapters 2 through 7 highlight salient motifs in the practice of fasting in the respective religions. Chapter 8 identifies some values that emerge universally, and chapter 9 responds to some frequently asked questions from those who are motivated to integrate this age-old practice into their spiritual lives today.

Fasting, then, as we will be using the term, is an intentional abstention from food and drink on *religious* grounds. The meaning of fasting in this discussion is grasped only if it is seen as an act essentially of the religious spirit.

The person who fasts stands in a noble tradition. In the religious experience of humankind, fasting has always been a prelude and means to a deeper spiritual life. Failure to control the amount we eat and drink disturbs the inner order of our body-spirit. Fasting is a choice to abstain from food at certain times in order to put our attention on something more important to us than ourselves or our sensory appetites.

Our unlimited freedoms and resources have not brought us unlimited fulfillment. The time has come for the consumer society to generate its antithesis: the person who stands against the conditioned reflex, who is free not to consume, who chooses to fast because of the self-transcending meaning and values perceived. May these pages open a door for you to ancient treasure awaiting rediscovery.

A NOTE ON THE TEXT

The New Revised Standard Version translation is used for quotations from the Bible, except where noted. Citations from the Bible and other Scriptures are added to the body of the text. In order to preserve the flavor of the Scriptures from various traditions and the voices of the people who contributed their own thoughts to this book, their original language has been maintained whenever possible, including instances of masculine God language.

CHAPTER ONE

IN SEARCH OF FASTING AS A SPIRITUAL PRACTICE

I grew up in a Catholic family in a small town of 1,200 called Bird Island in southern Minnesota. I first learned about fasting in 1953, when I was in the second grade and preparing for my first Holy Communion. When we were going to receive Communion at Mass, we were not to eat or drink anything from midnight of the evening before. Mothers were known to tie towels around the water faucets in the kitchen and bathroom so that the children would remember and not break their fast by drinking water. My religion teacher at school said that not eating or drinking was to help build up our anticipation of meeting Jesus.

Fridays were different. On Fridays throughout the year, everyone seven years of age and older abstained from meat or any products made from meat. My sister and I rather liked the abstinence days. Her supper favorites on those days were macaroni and cheese or deviled eggs and cheese; mine were creamed tuna on toast or fish sticks toasted in the oven.

On Ash Wednesday and Fridays in Lent, the grownups (those between twenty-one and fifty-nine) had to watch how much they ate because they could have just one full meal with two other little ones. Actually, they could have only one full meal a day on *all* the weekdays during Lent, although they could eat meat if it wasn't Friday. My parents said we abstained from meat on Fridays as a little reminder of how much Jesus loved us in giving his life for us on the cross. It was our way of saying that we were sorry for our sins and that we wanted to show our appreciation for being forgiven them by doing something out of love for him.

There were a few other fast days in the year like the Fridays in Lent; they came the day before the big feast days such as Christmas, Pentecost, All Saints' Day, or the Assumption of Mary. When my mother announced one of those days outside Lent, you knew the church was going to be extra full the next day.

The Second Vatican Council convened by Pope John XXIII in 1962 spanned my final years in high school and first year in college. My religion teachers in those years described it as the most important church meeting in a hundred years, and they all seemed to be waiting with some excitement to see what would come out of it. It didn't take long for the anticipated changes to begin happening in ways that altered our religious practices. The reorganization of church rules with regard to fasting (only one full meal a day) and abstinence (no meat) was a case in point.

Shortly after the council ended, on February 17, 1966, Pope Paul VI issued an apostolic constitution entitled *Poenitemini* (On Fast and Abstinence) revamping the existing discipline. Abstinence from meat and meat products, it said, was to be observed on every Friday, and fast as well as abstinence on Ash Wednesday and Good Friday. The new rules changed the age at which Catholics should begin to observe abstinence from seven to fourteen years and changed the age at which they ceased to be obliged by the law of fasting to their sixtieth year. More significantly, Pope Paul authorized bishops' conferences to adapt the laws to suit modern conditions and to emphasize prayer and works of charity as substitutes for previous practices of abstinence and fasting.

In November of that same year, the U.S. bishops did adapt the laws. They weren't saying that fasting wasn't important anymore. The message was that fasting was *so* important that it had to be rescued from the legalism, minimalism, and externalism into which it had fallen. The bishops followed up the pope's document with a pastoral statement that recommended that Catholics continue *voluntarily* to observe *some* acts of penance (not necessarily fasting) on *all* Fridays of the year. While Friday abstinence from meat was itself not going to be required by law (except during Lent), Fridays were singled out as days on which we should try to give special expression to our everyday call to love by entering into some other related activities. "It would bring great glory to God and good to souls," they wrote, "if Fridays found our people doing volunteer work in hospitals, visiting the sick, serving the needs of the aged and lonely, instructing the young in the faith, participating as Christians in community affairs, and meeting obligations to families, friends, neighbors, and parish with special zeal."

Most Catholics, myself among them, got the part about some obligation being taken away, but most also seemed to miss the part about something positive being put in its place, that is, that abstinence and fast, still valuable, could be replaced wholly or in part with other forms of penitence, works of charity, and exercises of piety. Neither Pope Paul nor the U.S. bishops intended to de-emphasize the value of penitential practice. Rather, they underlined it in red. But they did it in a way that Roman Catholics hadn't been reared to appreciate, by *removing* the laws instead of putting more laws there. They challenged people to rediscover the spirit of penitential practice and to find the forms that would give meaningful expression to the appropriate sentiments of the heart. Recognizing that the laws of fast and abstinence had all too often become rote observances, the bishops called upon their people to see that the Lenten fast and Friday abstinence were not necessarily the most effective means of expressing repentence. Visiting old Mrs. Meier in the nursing home might be a lot harder and actually do some good.

I was just in my second year of college in New Jersey by the time these changes, among others, were announced. Some clear shifts in emphasis were occurring. The leadership was summoning us to be adults in the faith, to act responsibly and with awareness. The approach to the practice of fasting reflected this shift. Whereas the Roman Catholic Church used to stress *both* the need for and the how-to details of this spiritual life tool, it was now choosing just to reaffirm the need and leave the details up to its members. Previously, the faithful, as one of my former high school teachers commented recently, didn't have the right to have an opinion about it: "We just obeyed the church laws. It was an obligation imposed upon us, and we just did it."

Now the church was asking its members to give the practice some thought and to use the tools of the spiritual life that fit their needs and situation and that effectively expressed their inner conversion of heart. Had this change come all by itself, it might have gotten more attention and been better interpreted to the faithful at the parish level. It was instead just one of a broad range of changes that resulted from the council and that altered the face of the church—from the language and order of its worship, to the increased role of the laity in parish ministries, to the daily devotional practices of the members. New directives were coming from the bishop's office for announcement on Sundays. The clergy didn't have adequate opportunity in their middle-management positions to digest and assimilate for themselves the renewal taking place, much less interpret it effectively for their faithful. There was a fresh wind blowing, a spirit of experimentation and emancipation, and in retrospect it's not surprising that a lot of the interpretive details and nuances got lost in the shuffle.

New Discoveries

After teaching English literature and religion and coaching football and track for a couple of years in a southern California high school, I decided to join the Paulists, a community of priests in the Roman Catholic Church, and began formal studies in theology in Washington, D.C. Our seminary community mirrored in every way the flux taking place in the church. The traditional devotional practices were looked upon by the students by and large as passé, and whatever was new, original, and creative easily won our attention.

It was difficult to transcend the optimism and energy of the era because it permeated the air like sunlight on a clear day. But, amid all the experimentation, it also left us without secure moorings in our spiritual life practices. Beyond the daily celebration of the Eucharist, each of us was largely left to assemble for himself a coherent set of practices that would support him in a life of ministry. I had taken a leave, like most other members of my church, from fasting and abstinence as regular disciplines of the spiritual life.

My first assignment after ordination in 1975 was to the Catholic Student Center at the Ohio State University in Columbus. A Day of Fast for World Hunger, sponsored by the university campus ministry, provided me with a new experience in fasting. It was the first time I had ever gone a whole day without food. There was a prayer vigil that evening at which people gave the money that they would have spent on food that day. Half of it went to a neighborhood soup kitchen for the homeless, and the other half went to the organization Bread for the World. I remember that I had a headache when I went home that evening, but I was even more aware that something in the experience had touched my heart and left me with intimations of a power in fasting that I wanted to explore further.

So I began to keep my eyes open for books about fasting. It was a revelation to me that so many of the things people said in them had no necessary or explicit connection to God. There was obviously a significant side to this practice that I had simply missed, and the things I read only deepened my interest. There were statements such as:

> I fast to pull the loose ends together in my life.
> I used to do a lot of things that were at cross-purposes with my own health and well-being. Fasting introduced me to a more genuinely life-supporting way to live.
> Since I've been fasting, I'm more sensitive to what messages are coming from both my heart and my body.
> About a year ago I began fasting one day a week. It's been the most settled, healthy, productive year of my life.

More people were apparently practicing voluntary fasting than I would ever have guessed. And these people who said they normally feel just "so-so" or "okay" claimed to be feeling abundantly alive. Even more impressive was that they were from all ages and backgrounds: athletes, musicians, students, teachers, union leaders, clergy, medical professionals, artists, construction workers, designers, writers, photographers, secretaries, actors, bus drivers, and store managers. If you were to believe these health books, the rediscovery of fasting was like a great awakening that was cutting across all societal lines and claiming followers from every sector of human experience.

I wanted to know more about what motivated this. Of the several reasons that repeatedly surfaced in the literature, though not all of them motivated every person who fasted, the reason most often cited as a motivational factor was what one might call "body-ecology." Many people said they fasted simply to give their physical selves a rest, a holiday. The argument went like this: The body is constantly absorbed in the work of digesting food, metabolizing it into energy, and eliminating the waste materials. To go without eating from time to time is to reward our bodies with the same kind of vacation that we give our minds after we've been working hard at reading or writing. Our bodies have lots of tasks to accomplish: digestion, elimination, fighting diseases, replenishing worn-out cells, and rejuvenating the blood. Of these, one of the most taxing is digestion. When we stop putting food into the body for a time, some of the other important internal concerns receive more attention. Fasting, in short, gives the body a chance to renew itself. It is a time in which the body burns its rubbish. It's like housecleaning day.

It was an approach emblematic of the seventies, an era of consciousness-raising in the domain of personal health, a decade that gave us the "Thank You for Not Smoking" buttons and witnessed the proliferation of health-food stores and the rise of jogging and cross-country skiing. Should it come as any surprise, then, that as people discovered that fasting is healthy, more and more would be interested in trying it and wanting to know more about it? The list of motivating factors was both long and impressive:

To lose weight the quickest and easiest way
To feel better physically and mentally
To look and feel younger
To save money
To give the whole system a rest
To clean out the body
To lower blood pressure and cholesterol levels
To cut down on smoking and drinking
To get more out of sex
To let the body heal itself
To relieve tension
To end dependence on drugs
To sleep better
To digest food better
To regulate the bowels

To feel euphoric
To sharpen the senses
To quicken mental processes
To save time
To boost self-esteem
To learn better eating habits
To share with the hungry
To gain control of oneself
To call attention to social issues
To slow the aging process

In Search of a Holistic Approach

Those reasons, of course, were the ones cited in the books on the "health" shelf of the bookstore. In the other literature—the pamphlets in the church bookstores or in the rack at the back of the church—it was all about God, and usually in a Lenten framework. There was a major disconnect in the two kinds of literature I was surveying. The material from the health-food store gave you the body-ecology approach and that from the church the spirituality approach. What I did not find were books or articles that helped people to integrate the physical *and* the spiritual benefits of fasting. It doesn't have to be either/or, I told myself. It can and should be both, because we are not just bodies and we are not just spirits. We are embodied spirits. Enspirited flesh. What is good for me physically is good for me. And what is good for me spiritually is good for me. There's only one "me" to which it all comes back.

And confining a means of spiritual growth to the six weeks of Lent made no sense either. If it was a valuable practice for those six weeks, then it should have something of value in it to recommend it for the other forty-six weeks of the year. As a spiritual life practice, it did not make sense to box it up and write "Lent" on it. Either it was potentially supportive for Christian *life* throughout the year, or it could be dispensed with without great loss in Lent.

I decided to explore these questions further by preparing and promoting a (what else?) Lenten Bible study series called "The Adventure of Fasting" at our campus ministry center. The title itself increased the participation; whatever experience people had of fasting, it hadn't been an "adventure"! We began with a survey of all the passages on fasting in the Bible. Then we talked a good deal about its human roots in the virtues of moderation and temperance. This is the place, we felt, from which the project of developing a holistic vision of fasting's benefits must begin—with an appreciation of the virtue of temperance. Temperance is like a chain with a hook on each end: One end attaches to physiological health, the other end to spiritual health. The chain goes out in both directions and links the two because temperance has implications for the health and wholeness of your embodied spirit taken as a whole. Temperance is the genus, fasting the species; temperance is the game, fasting the player; temperance is the book, fasting the chapter.

We strove to articulate a holistic approach, one dealing with the human person as an embodied spirit. On the one hand, we wanted to rediscover the value of fasting as an act of faith, hope, and love, a religious act, directed toward God. We saw in the tradition how people fasted to focus the heart, turned to it as a behavior that clears away the thousand little things that clutter the mind. We saw it as an action that renews contact with God, like removing the rust and corrosion from a car battery to enable the current to flow more freely.

On the other hand, we wanted to recognize the physiological dimension, too. There is a lot of clutter and excess that could be removed from our bodies with benefit. The body has accumulated a lot of mucus and toxins and drugs and chemicals that, if unloaded, would enable the vital current of life to flow through us much more freely. The temptation is to label the former one as "spiritual" and the latter as "physical," the one as good for my soul, and the other as good for my body. But it's all *me*. And, therefore, it's all related. It is with my *self,* my embodied spirit, that I respond to God. If my digestive system is weighed down, blocked, overloaded, lethargic, that's going to influence my heart response to God concerning my experience of the goodness of life. If I feel awful for physiological reasons, God is not likely to get many outpourings of joy and praise from my mouth. But if I feel that every physical thing is running smoothly, if I feel the energy is flowing, if I feel calm and peaceful with myself, productive and useful to others, and—well—*healthy,* then how much more easily prayer will come!

Our Bible study series was an event in which we looked again at a practice that had been observed in our earlier years and then swept away. In critiquing our society's tendency to permissiveness and overindulgence, we were like a person who, sated with food to the point of discomfort, decides that it may feel better not to eat so much. In short, we were ready to fast. Unable to find a holistic resource on the subject that dealt with fasting as a seamless unity, I wrote my own and titled it *Fasting Rediscovered: A Guide to Health and Wholeness for Your Body-Spirit.*[1]

It has been said that what the parents throw away as useless, the children bring back as newfound treasure. What one generation discards, the other generation unearths and enshrines. I emerged from that series of discussions with a fresh appreciation for fasting as a way of communicating with God and as a way of caring for our enspirited bodies. Shortly thereafter, I started fasting one day a week. It was the beginning of a journey that continues into the present, one in which my own practice has been enriched and challenged by what I have learned from fasting in other religions.

FEAR NOT: IT WON'T KILL YOU

If you are coming new to the subject, allow me, at the outset, to anticipate the slightest twinge of a normal reaction that you may encounter within yourself: "Me fast? I don't want to die!"

Underlying that understandable reaction is a confusion between fasting and starvation. Let's dispel that confusion right away. Fasting is a positive, freely chosen action that bestows a number of benefits. Starving, in contrast, is usually an involuntary wasting away through the prolonged unavailability of food or inadequate amounts of food.

The derivations of the words themselves are instructive. The word *fast* derives from *faestan* (Old English, meaning "to abstain"). The abstention is voluntary and undertaken for good effects. It is life-enhancing. The word *starvation* comes from the Old English *sterofan,* a derivation of the Teutonic verb *sterben,* which means "to die." As I will explain more fully in chapter 9, "Preparing to Practice," when we fast, we in effect decide that we are going to take our nourishment from the reserves we have been storing up. Starvation begins when the storage shelves have been emptied, when the body has consumed its spare resources, craves food, and continues to be deprived.

It is essential to clear up straightaway the misconception that fasting is the same as starvation. They represent entirely different periods in the process of abstaining from food. The fasting stage continues so long as the body supports itself on the stored reserves within its tissues. Starvation begins when abstinence is carried beyond the time when these stored reserves are used up or have dropped to a dangerously low level. It takes a very long fast—much longer than anything we'll be considering in these pages—to cross the line into starvation. The body has some finely tuned warning systems that give the signal when it is time to break a fast. That time does not generally occur until somewhere between thirty and forty days, which is far, far longer than the kinds of fasts proposed by the various religions whose fasting practices are presented in this book.

We live in a society that practically equates "three squares a day" with the preservation of life itself. We live with a mistaken notion that to miss a meal or two would be hazardous to our health and well-being. We don't, however, have as grave a problem with overeating. That, we rationalize, allows us to store up reserves for that "emergency situation" when we may have to miss a meal. What we have yet to understand is that the body tolerates a fast far better than a feast. It has ample resources to nourish itself for surprisingly long periods of time.

What could be more reassuring than to know that fasting, the partial or total abstinence from food and drink, is found in virtually every religion from primitive to modern times and practiced for a variety of reasons? The wisdom contained in the religious traditions of the world about fasting is, ironically, a rich feast.

CHAPTER TWO

JUDAISM: PURIFICATION, MOURNING, ATONEMENT

Biblical Judaism and the Judaism of today are two very different forms of religion. In the first half of this chapter I will be dealing largely with biblical Judaism. In the second half, living voices from the tradition describe contemporary practice.

The Hebrews, the Aramaeans, the Arabs, and the Ethiopians all used the same word for fasting, a word that appears in both early and late Hebrew Bible writings: *tsoum*. In modern Hebrew the word is *Ta'anit*. The word in its first level of meaning signifies "withholding all natural food from the body," especially for a religious purpose. The second level of meaning includes an expression of sorrow for sins and a penitential offering. Together they convey the idea of voluntary deprivation of the bodily appetites for the purpose of orienting the human spirit to God.

The two "summit" experiences in the Hebrew scriptures of encounters with God are those of Moses and Elijah. For both, the encounter took place on Mount Sinai and was preceded by a fast of forty days and forty nights—on the mountain covered in a cloud for Moses (Exod. 34:28) and in the desert for Elijah (1 Kings 19:8). For each, the fast was marked by a spirit of preparation. In Moses's case, the drama created by the construction and worship of the golden calf during his first visitation on the mountain required two fasts and two meetings, the first in preparation, the second to make amends for the sin of idolatry committed by his people:

> So I turned and went down from the mountain, while the mountain was ablaze; the two tablets of the covenant were in my two hands. Then I saw that you had indeed sinned against the Lord your God, by casting for yourselves an image of a calf; you had been quick to turn from the way that the Lord had commanded you. So I took hold of the two tablets and flung them from my two hands, smashing them before your eyes. Then I lay prostrate before the Lord as before, forty days and forty nights; I neither ate bread nor drank water, because of all the sin you had committed, provoking the Lord by doing what was evil in his sight. (Deut. 9:15–18)

MOTIFS IN THE JEWISH PRACTICE OF FASTING

From Moses's encounters with the Divine Presence comes the Torah and within it Mosaic Law, with its pervasive concern for purity in the presence of God; the dietary laws that evolved were but one expression of this. Jewish tradition is that Moses delivered the Torah to the people, with some 613 positive and negative commandments in it. The Torah provides rules or laws that guide our lives; much attention is paid to specific instructions. The Book of Leviticus, for example, provides guidelines for ritual and sacrificial practice. The Book of Deuteronomy repeats and explains the instructions as proclaimed to Moses on Sinai. Proper practice of the instructions ensured a continued and prosperous communion with God. The Torah provides a variety of circumstances to which fasting was deemed the appropriate response.

First, as purification in preparation for some religious duty. Moses remained fasting on Sinai for forty days and nights when about to receive the Ten Commandments (Exod. 34:28), and Daniel fasted for a considerable time seeking to know God's will (Dan. 9:3; 10:2). As a duty to her people, Esther agreed to see King Ahasuerus uninvited, and she asked the Jewish people to fast for three days beforehand (Esther 4:16).

Second, as an accompaniment or manifestation of mourning. David and his followers, for example, "mourned and wept and fasted until evening for Saul and his son Jonathan, and for the army of the Lord and for the house of Israel, because they had fallen by the sword" (2 Sam. 1:12). The fact that David did *not* fast after the death of the child he had fathered with Bathsheba caused surprise in his attendants, which suggests that the usual procedure was to fast after a death as an expression of mourning and loss. So it is not surprising to read that when Abner was buried in Hebron, the people went to "console David with food while it was still day, but David swore, 'May God do thus and so to me if I eat anything else before sunset'" (2 Sam. 3:32–35).

Third, as an act of repentance and atonement to conciliate God. Illustrations of this are numerous: Ahab fasted to avert the disaster predicted by Elijah (1 Kings 21:27–29); Nehemiah fasted over the sad condition of Jerusalem (Neh. 1:4); and the whole people fasted in times of peril and misfortune (2 Chron. 20:3; Jer. 36:9). "So they gathered at Mizpah, and drew water and poured it out before the Lord. They fasted that day and said, 'We have sinned against the Lord'" (1 Sam 7:6).

THE DAY OF ATONEMENT

The Torah obliged the people to observe only one day of fasting in the year: Yom Kippur, the Day of Atonement (Lev. 23:26ff). On that day, the tenth day of the seventh month *(Tishri),* the high priest sent a scapegoat out into the desert, symbolically laden with the sins of the people, who meanwhile were fasting in prayer that God would take from his sight their sins as individuals and as a nation. This day of fasting was taken very seriously: Anyone who decided to satisfy his or her own hunger pains on this day was cut off from the community.

Yom Kippur is one of the most observed holidays in the Jewish year. Many Jews who do not observe other Jewish customs will refrain from work, fast, and attend synagogue services on this day. It is a day of spiritual renewal and critical self-examination when people atone for the sins of the past year, a last chance to demonstrate repentance and to make amends. To atone for sins against another person, you must seek reconciliation with that person. Yom Kippur is lived as a complete Sabbath. It is a complete twenty-five-hour fast beginning at sunset on the evening before Yom Kippur and ending after nightfall on the day itself. The Talmud mentions additional restrictions, including those against washing and bathing, anointing your body (using cosmetics), and engaging in sexual relations. Anyone whose health will be harmed by fasting is not permitted to fast.

Most of the day is spent in the synagogue in prayer. Services end at nightfall with a long blast on the *shofar*. It is Orthodox tradition to wear white on the holiday, symbolic of purity and a reminder of God's promise: "Come now, let us argue it out, says the Lord: though your sins are like scarlet, they shall be like snow; though they are red like crimson, they shall become like wool" (Isa. 1:18). Yom Kippur expresses one of the major reasons for fasting in Judaism: *teshuvah,* or "return"—to return to God and to our essential state of purity before God.

Why is it that prayers of repentance are accompanied by depriving the body of food? The question finds no definitive answer in Torah. Some believe that nothing is more natural. It is by a profound and spontaneous movement of their whole being that religious people stand before God in their limitations and sinfulness. They deprive themselves because they exceeded themselves. To fast is an act of humility, an act of remembering who you are in relation to God.

THE FASTS OF MOURNING

One of the distinctive characteristics of fasting in Judaism is the selection of days that commemorate calamities in war, the destruction of the First and Second Temples, the assassination of leaders, the Holocaust, and the death of loved ones. Judaism is the only religion in which fasting is directly tied to the recollection of tragedies in the people's history.

The Jewish lunar calendar is based on the revolutions of the moon around the earth every 29.5 days; the months alternate between 29 and 30 days in length. The second major fast day in Judaism comes on the ninth *(Tish'ah)* day of the month of *Av* and is referred to as Tisha B'Av. It is a fast of mourning. The historical context is the conquest of Jerusalem and the destruction of the First Temple, the Temple of Solomon, in 586 BCE by Nebuchadnezzar, king of Babylonia. On Tisha B'Av the Book of Lamentations is chanted with a unique minor melody. Historically, the congregation sat on the floor, forgoing the comfort of chairs.

After the Persians conquered the Babylonians, King Cyrus of Persia gave permission to the exiles to return to Judea. The Temple was rebuilt in the fifth century BCE, and this Second Temple remained standing until it was destroyed in 70 CE by the Romans. The destruction of the Second Temple also occurred on the ninth of *Av*, thereby giving another layer of meaning to the motif of mourning on this day.

The destruction of the Second Temple was a watershed event in Jewish history. It effectively ended the Temple cult. Since then, the Judaism we know today is rabbinic Judaism, the Judaism crystallized and carried forward by the sages and Rabbis, the heirs of the Pharisees. The sages mandated the people to pray, "May God allow the restoration of the Temple in our days," although they had laid the groundwork for Judaism as a spiritual discipline with no need for the Temple.

There are variations in the ways Jews practice fasting. On Tisha B'Av, Orthodox Jews fast from just before sunset to the following evening; more liberal Jews end the fast after the early afternoon service to express their belief that the establishment of the State of Israel is the spiritual equivalent to the rebuilding of the Temple of Solomon.

There are also five minor fasts on the Jewish calendar (the Hebrew names for the months are given in parentheses below), two of them relating to the siege that resulted in the eventual destruction of the First Temple.

- The Fast of Tevet (*Tevet* 10) marks the beginning of the siege of Jerusalem by Nebuchadnezzar.
- The Fast of Tammuz (*Tammuz* 17) marks the date when the walls of Jerusalem were breached by Nebuchadnezzar's Babylonian forces. This day is the beginning of the Three Weeks, an annual period of mourning over the destruction of the First and Second Temples in Jerusalem.
- The Fast of Gedaliah (*Tishri* 3) recalls the killing of Gedaliah, the Jewish governor of Judah, a critical event in the downfall of the royal dynasty of Judah.
- The Fast of Esther (*Adar* 13) commemorates the three days that Esther and the people fasted before she approached the king of Persia on behalf of her people.
- The Fast of the Firstborn (*Nisan* 14) is observed only by firstborn males, recalling that they were saved from the plague of the firstborn in Egypt. It is observed on the day preceding Passover.

These five minor fasts last from dawn to nightfall, whereas the fasts for Yom Kippur and Tisha B'Av begin at sunset and end the following day when the first three stars can be seen. On the minor fast days, breakfast may be taken before sunrise. On all seven, adult Jews may neither eat nor drink, even water. As in the major fasts, a great deal of leniency is allowed in these minor fasts for people with medical conditions or other obstacles to fasting. Charitable giving, especially the distribution of food necessary for the evening meal, is encouraged. If any of the minor fast dates falls on the Sabbath, when fasting is not permitted, it is deferred to the following day.

Besides these fixed fast days, there are some other fasts that are local or regional. These fasts, too, are related to unfortunate occurrences or disasters in the history of the Jewish people. Historically, each individual synagogue may impose fasting on its congregation in the case of a misfortune befalling the people in its community.

Private fasts are also observed among Jews. The bride and groom may fast on the day before their wedding to review and renew their lives. When the married couple share a cup of wine under the wedding canopy, the fast ends. Other private fasting rituals, though rare, can be highly personal: A person might fast after experiencing a bad dream, believing it will assist in restoring joy; on the anniversary of the death of a close relative; on certain days either in memory of particular events in their own lives or in expiation for their sins or to beg God's mercy in time of trouble. There are some examples in Jewish history, usually related to Jewish mysticism, of extreme fasts being undertaken to achieve visions, but on the whole mainstream Judaism has been set against such practices. If anything, the rabbinic tradition offers moderating examples of rabbis forbidding a fast in the case of a scholar who would be disturbed in his study, or of a teacher who would thereby be prevented from doing his work properly.

Private, penitential fasting is also practiced in Judaism. Some devout people promise to fast in three-day regimens such as Monday-Thursday-Monday for a number of weeks, for example during the winter weeks when the first eight Torah portions of Exodus are read in the synagogue. In mystical circles, there is also a fast of speaking, during which the penitent spends a certain number of days in silence.[2]

THE PURPOSE OF FASTING

What is clear when we look at the practice of fasting in Judaism (as well as in the other Abrahamic religions of Christianity and Islam) is that it's about *relationship.* In Jewish practice, sometimes the emphasis is on atonement, at other times on purification or mourning, but it is always about *connecting* with the Holy One through fasting. There is a passage in the book of the prophet Ezekiel that colorfully and poignantly illustrates how God is a personal, passionate presence to the people of Israel:

> The word of the Lord came to me: Mortal, make known to Jerusalem her abominations, and say, Thus says the Lord God to Jerusalem: Your origin and your birth were in the land of the Canaanites; your father was an Amorite, and your mother a Hittite. As for your birth, on the day you were born your navel cord was not cut, nor were you washed with water to cleanse you, nor rubbed with salt, nor wrapped in cloths. No eye pitied you, to do any of these things for you out of compassion for you; but you were thrown out in the open field, for you were abhorred on the day you were born.
>
> I passed by you, and saw you flailing about in your blood. As you lay in your blood, I said to you, "Live! And grow up like a plant of the field." You grew up and became tall and arrived at full womanhood; your breasts were formed, and your hair had grown; yet you were naked and bare.
>
> I passed by you again and looked on you; you were at the age for love. I spread the edge of my cloak over

you, and covered your nakedness: I pledged myself to
you and entered into a covenant with you, says the Lord
God, and you became mine. Then I bathed you with
water and washed off the blood from you, and anointed
you with oil. I clothed you with embroidered cloth and
with sandals of fine leather; I bound you in fine linen and
covered you with rich fabric. I adorned you with orna-
ments: I put bracelets on your arms, a chain on your
neck, a ring on your nose, earrings in your ears, and a
beautiful crown upon your head. You were adorned with
gold and silver, while your clothing was of fine linen,
rich fabric, and embroidered cloth. You had choice flour
and honey and oil for food. You grew exceedingly beautiful, fit to be a queen. Your fame spread among the
nations on account of your beauty, for it was perfect
because of my splendor that I had bestowed on you, says
the Lord God. But you trusted in your beauty, and
played the whore because of your fame, and lavished
your whorings on any passerby....

Yet I will remember my covenant with you in the
days of your youth, and I will establish with you an ever-
lasting covenant, and you shall know that I am the Lord,
in order that you may remember and be confounded, and
may never open your mouth again because of your shame,
when I forgive you all that you have done, says the Lord.
(Ezek. 16:1–15, 60, 63)

The imagery and language of this passage provide a context
for the Israelites' use of fasting. It reveals a terribly moving, personal, and profound relationship between the people of Israel
and God. There is no sense of remoteness here. No sense of a
God who winds up the world like a clock and walks off to leave
it ticking on its own. They are not fasting to an abstraction.
Their fasting is an expression of their awareness that they are in

relationship with one who sees their hearts. Whereas the women of our time have been known to lay out an elegant meal to get to the heart of their beloved, we see Esther, Judith, and Sarah employing a reverse tactic: They *fast* to move God to grant them a desired favor.

There is something so vitally personal about this: Certainly a "God of the philosophers" would not be swayed by such wile and pressure. An "Unmoved Mover" would itself be likely to remain unmoved. A "First Cause" would surely be unaffected by such despicably emotional behavior. But the God of the Israelites is another story. Here is one who suffers fits of jealousy, who succumbs to possessiveness, who is enraged when the eyes of the betrothed begin to stray and linger upon the competition. It is not surprising to expect this God to be moved and affected when God's people sought attention in a deeply real and no-nonsense manner.

But when this sense of "heart to heart" waned and legalism crept in, three postexilic prophets verbally lashed out at those fasts that were filled with exterior ritual but lacked a genuine spirit of inner change.

> When you fasted and lamented in the fifth month and in the seventh, for these seventy years, was it for me that you fasted?... Thus says the Lord of hosts: Render true judgments, show kindness and mercy to one another; do not oppress the widow, the orphan, the alien, or the poor, and do not devise evil in your hearts against one another.
>
> (Zech. 7:5, 9, 10)

This passage from Isaiah 58:3–7 is perhaps the most familiar of all the examples of prophetic severity:

[People]
    Why do we fast, but you do not see? Why humble ourselves, but you do not notice?

[God]

Look, you serve your own interest on your fast day, and oppress all your workers.

Look, you fast only to quarrel and to fight and to strike with a wicked fist.

Such fasting as you do today will not make your voice heard on high.

Is such the fast that I choose, a day to humble oneself?

Is it to bow down the head like a bulrush, and to lie in sackcloth and ashes?

Will you call this a fast, a day acceptable to the Lord?

And then God goes on to stress the importance of the harmonious balance between fasting, doing good to others, and intimacy with God:

Is not this the fast that I choose: to loose the bonds of injustice,

to undo the thongs of the yoke, to let the oppressed go free, and to break every yoke?

Is it not to share your bread with the hungry, and to bring your homeless poor into your house; when you see the naked, to cover them, and not to hide yourself from your kin?

The overarching virtue in Judaism is fidelity to the Torah. Torah means "teaching," which sometimes is used narrowly to refer to the scroll containing the Five Books of Moses and sometimes is used more broadly to refer to the complete body of Hebrew Scripture. Under the umbrella of Torah we find certain recurring expressions of piety, like almsgiving (Lev. 23:22; Deut. 24:19–22), fasting (Joel 1:14; Lev. 16:29–34; 1 Sam. 14:24 and 31:13), and prayer (Exod. 20:3; Ps. 63:6–8). In the Temple days, worship mainly consisted of ritual sacrifice, as opposed to the contemporary rabbinical ideal of worship, communal prayer. Although these three ideals were seldom mentioned together, the proper practice of each demanded attention to the others. Just as Amos railed against ritual worship unaccompanied by justice (Amos 5:21–24), so did Isaiah cry out against fasting without justice. God requires that we devote ourselves in every way since it is devotion of the heart that is the critical agent in every activity.

> Yet even now, says the Lord, return to me with all your heart, with fasting, with weeping, and with mourning; rend your hearts and not your clothing. Return to the Lord, your God, for he is gracious and merciful, slow to anger and abounding in steadfast love, and relents from punishing. (Joel 2:12, 13)

These words of Zachary, Isaiah, and Joel make it unmistakably clear that in this new life with God, there is a hierarchy of values. Justice and mercy trump penance, the latter having no value without the former. These are the virtues that make fasting agreeable to God. "It is love that I desire, and not sacrifice" (Hosea 6:6). Love concretizes itself in an efficacious mercy that reaches out to the needy. Thus emerges a kind of triad: fasting, prayer, and works of mercy.

A LIVING VOICE FROM THE TRADITION

Every generation needs its prophetic voices. The challenge of keeping spiritual practices vibrant and on target with their original meaning is familiar to every religion. To this end, it is helpful to listen to two living voices from the tradition. The first belongs to Aliza Bulow, program director for The Jewish

Experience in Denver, Colorado, who works actively to keep the traditional practices meaningful today. As a teacher of practical Jewish philosophy through The Jewish Experience and Lishmah Woman's Torah Center, she has some contemporary responses to the age-old questions of: Why do we fast? What function does it serve in our spiritual life? How can being hungry and thirsty help us connect with God? She also identifies a holistic approach that is innate to Jewish understanding of the human person, wherein fasting is not just for either the body or the soul. There is just one entity: the enfleshed spirit, the animated body, the soul incarnated in a unified embodied spirit. She reflects on how the practice of fasting, in which the interior sorrow and conversion of the heart are expressed through the physical fast of abstaining from bodily food, admirably illustrate this unity.

> There are six regular fast days in the Jewish year (seven if you count the fast of the first born before Seder night). Two of these days, Tisha B'Av and Yom Kippur, are "full" fasts. They begin at sunset and end the following day when the stars appear. The rest are "half" day fasts, lasting from sunrise to stars out. During these times, adult Jews [defined as age thirteen] may neither eat nor drink—even water (there are exceptions for people with health issues).
>
> Except for Yom Kippur, these fast days were established because of the catastrophes and suffering that occurred on those dates. Their purpose is to help Jews today to recall the negative behavior of our ancestors that led to those calamities and to focus our attention on our own parallel behavior that continues to drive our nation into similar negative situations. During these days, each person is meant to make a personal accounting of his or her behavior and resolve to return to the positive path.
>
> According to Eliyahu Kitov in *The Book of Our Heritage,* one who fasts and spends the day idly without

repentance misses the point. That person is emphasizing the fasting, which is secondary, and de-emphasizing the repentance, which is primary. He quotes the book of Jonah (3:10) where it says about the people of the city of Nineveh, "And God saw their actions." Our sages point out that the verse doesn't say that God saw their sackcloth and fasting, but their actions (Babylonian Talmud, Ta'anit 22a). The purpose of fasting is to bring one to repent, and true repentance brings about a change in actions.

However, repenting without fasting is not enough. The fast days were ordained either in the Torah, by the prophets, or by the Rabbis throughout the generations, and they have been accepted and observed by the Jewish people. Since Judaism eschews asceticism for its own sake, there must be something unique about fasting that serves as a vehicle for repentance.

A distinctive feature of Judaism is its philosophy of integrating the spiritual with the physical. Jews do not reject the physical in favor of the spiritual; rather, they recognize the opportunity that living a physical existence provides for the exercise and strengthening of the spiritual. In this world, the physical and the spiritual are inextricably intertwined, and we must use both to activate our ultimate growth and to achieve our raison d'être.

We use the physical as a doorway through which we access the spiritual. This is one of the reasons that we clean the house, prepare delicious foods, and wear beautiful clothes for Shabbat. The sense of tranquility that stems from dwelling in an orderly environment, the fullness and pleasure that good food engenders, and the touch of majesty that we feel when dressed in our finery, all help create a sense of separation from the routine of the mundane and heighten our ability to connect to God. We manipulate the physical to gain access to the spiritual.

Hunger is a feeling of emptiness, of desire for sustenance. It can also refer to a non-food-related desire or craving, as in "hungry for success" or "hungry for power." One of Webster's definitions is "lacking needful or desirable elements; not fertile; poor." Hunger is the state of not having what we need (or want) and yearning for it.

Spiritual feelings are frequently very subtle; often, we have to put forth some effort to recognize them. *Halakhah* (traditional Jewish law) helps us in this process. By specifying particular behaviors and dictating when they must be performed, *Halakhah* provides physical sensations that point to spiritual realities.

Feeling hunger on a physical level helps us access the concept of desire and need on a spiritual level. Requiring fasting on days that necessitate repentance helps us activate the longing we have to walk on a path that leads to a rectified world. When employed, rather than ignored, the hunger can forward our repentance.

Fasting can also help us address the common difficulty of not relating to the reason for the fast day. Of course, educating ourselves as to the origin and significance of the day is vital, but even with an understanding of what the day is about, we can feel distant from its essence. Fasting helps engender a sense of loss and of vulnerability; with effort, these feelings can be used as steppingstones to internalizing the meanings of the events that prompted the declaration of that particular fast.

In addition, fasting is reminiscent of the atonement service that was performed in the Holy Temple in Jerusalem. During that time, one who sinned could activate his or her repentant energies by physically bringing an animal offering to God on the Temple altar. Of course God does not need offerings from humans; the entire process of animal sacrifices and offerings is about using the physical to access the spiritual. For some of the offerings, the fat and the blood of the animal would be consumed by fire (that part was "for" God), and the meat was eaten by people.

There is a very deep way that that process relates to fasting. In some Orthodox prayer books, there is a special prayer that is inserted at the end of the afternoon *Amidah* prayer on an individual fast day. The following is a loose translation:

> Master of the Universe, you know that during the time that the Holy Temple stood, a person who sinned could bring an offering, and nothing except the blood and fat was (actually) offered, and in Your great mercy, You would grant atonement. And now, I have fasted, and diminished my fat and my blood. May it be Your will that the diminishment of my fat and my blood, that was diminished today, be as if I offered it before you on the altar, and may you show me favor.

In other words, this prayer asks that the physical result of fasting be bound together with the spiritual impetus for fasting and that they be accepted by God as if they were offered in the time and place where we as a nation were most connected to God.

Fasting is difficult, but it is the very fact of its difficulty that gives us the opportunity to connect to God in a stronger way. The sublimation of our own desires to eat in favor of the directive to fast is itself an offering. In addition, harnessing the emptiness that fasting engenders to bring about a deeper level of repentance, along with the sacrifice that we can "offer" to God, makes fasting a precious opportunity for connecting ourselves with God's will.[3]

Rabbi Kerry M. Olitzky, executive director of the Jewish Outreach Institute, provides us with a second living voice from the tradition. Much of his rabbinate has been about helping individuals to reclaim Jewish ritual and understand its relevance in their own lives. He is the coeditor of *The Rituals and Practices of a Jewish Life: A Handbook for Personal Spiritual Renewal* (Jewish Lights) and the author of many books that bring Jewish wisdom into the everyday lives of people. His reflection on fasting in Judaism in my interview with him serves as an effective summary of the tradition in its contemporary expression in Jewish life.

For most Jews, fasting is a ritual act to be wrestled with prior to certain medical procedures and on Yom Kippur, the Day of Atonement, a holy day that occurs annually in the early fall (September or early October). Fasting is one of the salient elements of Yom Kippur's commemoration and concludes an extended period of nearly forty days of introspection and spiritual renewal. (It also concludes the more intensive ten-day period that begins with Rosh Hashanah, commonly known as the Days of Awe.) But Yom Kippur is only one of several days of fasting that take place during the Jewish religious calendar, all of which help to ready us for the more comprehensive fast of Yom Kippur. Thus, the fast on Yom Kippur is a culmination of the year's efforts, as much as it informs the spiritual practices during the year that follows it. The fast of Yom Kippur occurs at the beginning of the religious year as a way of helping us to prepare to meet the days ahead. In this way, fasting helps to center us as we face the challenges of daily living.

Fasting in Judaism is generally associated with mourning during perilous periods in Jewish history. In the Book of Esther, for example, the Jews of ancient Persia fasted and put on sackcloth and ashes in order to

change the decree against them made by King Ahasuerus.
Fasting is not required by mourners today, nor is it a practice generally undertaken to change the course of contemporary history. Instead, fasting is a sign of repentance,
an indication that we have changed our ways and are on
the path of spiritual renewal, on the road back to developing and maintaining a relationship with the Divine.
This is best described as part of the ongoing covenantal
relationship originally established between God and the
Jewish people on Sinai during the desert journey from
Egypt to Israel.

On Yom Kippur, we also fast as part of the process of
spiritual rebirthing. During Yom Kippur, we simulate
our own deaths in order to reawaken the spiritual self
that lies hidden beneath the surface of our being. To
emphasize this transition, traditional Jews wear a *kittel* [a
traditional shroud] on Yom Kippur. The wearing of this
ritual burial garment helps to further symbolize the
process of a spiritual death that must take place before a
rebirth can occur. Fasting also allows us to focus on the
transcendent values that guide our lives, rather than the
material pleasures that, as ironic as it sounds, seem to consume us—including the visceral pleasures associated with
eating. Fasting provides a spiritual foundation for
tzedakah (charitable giving), *tefillah* (prayer), and *teshuvah*
(return or repentance) as a way, according to Jewish theology, to limit the severity of the decree meted out on
Yom Kippur (namely, who is to live and who is to die
during the year ahead).

The fast on Yom Kippur is a major fast, so called
because it includes the cessation of eating and drinking for
the entire twenty-five-hour period (from sunset one day to
sundown on the day following). Such a major fast only takes
place during one other time of the year: Tisha B'Av (late July

or early August), which marks the destruction of the ancient Temple in Jerusalem and the concurrent dispersion of the Jewish people. Tisha B'Av also marks other major catastrophes from Jewish history. Other fasts that mark less significant historical events are designated as "minor," because they require that food and drink be avoided only during the hours of daylight.

Of course, there have been groups of people who sought to combine their sense of the spiritual with fasting. Thus, they fasted regularly even when the calendar did not call for it. For example, those who sought mystical visions often fasted for extensive periods of time while focusing on selected texts from the Psalms. These "chariot mystics," as they were called (a reference to the prophet Ezekiel's vision of the chariot), used psalm texts as *kavannot* (sacred mantras), and fasting became part of their regular spiritual practices. While there are few, if any, who precisely mimic such practices today, some elements have woven themselves into today's spiritual practice of Judaism.

All Jewish adults are required to fast. Jewish law defines adulthood as one who has reached the legal age of majority (traditionally designated as thirteen for boys and twelve for girls). However, some fasts, such as the fast of the firstborn during the day before the Passover Seder, is incumbent on only those firstborn members of the family. (This is traditionally designated as the first male issued from the womb, although some liberal Jewish women have taken on this obligation as well.) In addition, traditional brides and grooms regularly fast on the day of their wedding. In traditional circles, the groom wears the same *kittel* worn on Yom Kippur for similar reasons. The wedding also represents a rebirth—the transition of living as a single adult to the coupling of marriage. Mystics even suggest that the wedding is a return to the primordial state of life when souls were coupled. At birth, souls are split apart and then spend their days looking for their other halves. In all cases, those whose health would be compromised by fasting are not only exempt from fasting, they are required to eat. Thus, it would be a transgression of Jewish law for those exempted to fast.

While there are vast numbers of Jews who do not regularly practice Judaism in a traditional manner, an overwhelming number make sure that they find a way to the synagogue for worship services at least once a year on Yom Kippur. And while there are other rituals that are practiced more widely (such as the Passover Seder) among so-called unaffiliated Jews, many Jews do fast for some period of time on Yom Kippur—even if they neglect other rituals and less significant fast days during the rest of the year. While fasting itself looks the same for all branches of religious Judaism, particularly on Yom Kippur, the more liberal religious movements have historically not accepted the rationale behind fasting days other than Yom Kippur.

For example, the Reform movement chose not to mourn the destruction of the ancient Temple (on Tisha B'Av) because traditional Judaism explained it (and the consequent "exile" from Jerusalem) as punishment for the misdeeds of the Jewish people. Nor does the Reform movement anticipate a return to the sacrificial Temple cult once the messianic era is upon us, another aspect of traditional Jewish theology. Further, the Reform movement eventually saw no need to mourn the destruction of Jerusalem once the modern State of Israel was established.

Nevertheless, many liberal Jews fast on such days as I do as a way of getting in sync with the spiritual rhythm of the Jewish religious calendar. I also see fasting on such days as a way of focusing my attention on the general malaise of the period of time being remembered—hoping that it might be an inspiration for all of us and our time as well. It is also my way to remember those whom much of the world has forgotten. When the Temple was destroyed, many of my ancestors were killed. In a metaphysical way, fasting helps me to establish a direct spiritual connection with them.

While some may consider fasting a form of self-inflicted punishment, deprivation, or denial, I find the regular practice of fasting rather liberating. During specific periods of time, fasting provides me with the opportunity to move the focus of my attention away from my body (which does occupy me, as it does most others, a great deal of the time). If my physical exercise is the way to keep my body healthy and daily prayer keeps my soul in shape, then my regular practice of fasting helps to secure that link between them.

CHAPTER THREE

CHRISTIANITY: MYSTICAL LONGING, LIBERATION THROUGH DISCIPLINE, WORK OF JUSTICE

There are three major themes in the history and practice of Christian fasting: mystical union and longing for fulfillment, liberation through discipline (or penance), and the relationship of fasting to works of charity and justice. They are like three complementary strands in a weaving, with one or another in greater evidence at different historical periods and in different regions of the church. This chapter will present the spirituality impregnating each one and offer a reflection at the end on their relative applicability for our times.

MYSTICAL UNION AND LONGING FOR FULFILLMENT

Jesus begins his public life with a fast similar to that of Moses and Elijah: forty days and forty nights in a deserted place. This fact alone is significant because he teaches as much by his acts as by his words. Yet, he instituted no determinable practice for his followers; in fact, once into his ministry, he "came eating and drinking," so that some said of him, "Look, he is a glutton and a drunkard" (Luke 7:34). When Jesus's disciples asked him why they were not able to drive a demon from an epileptic, his response, according to an early Vulgate translation of the Bible, was, "This kind can only come out through prayer and fasting" (Mark 9:29). But biblical scholars today consider the phrase "and fasting" a later addition and generally cite it only in the footnotes as a variant, a reading supported by the same incident in Matthew's Gospel where the sentence does not appear at all. So we are left with the example of Jesus in the desert and the universal experience of the saints to indicate that prayer and fasting form the normal way of triumphing over evil spirits. On the face of it, both Jesus and Paul, while embracing the practice of fasting themselves, refrain from making it a requirement for their followers. Jesus explains this seeming paradox in responding to a question as to why his disciples don't fast like those of John the Baptist:

> The wedding guests cannot mourn as long as the bridegroom is with them, can they? The days will come when the bridegroom is taken away from them, and then they will fast. (Matt. 9:15)

At the very least one could say that this response indicates fasting is appropriate in the bridegroom's absence, but there is much more here than that. Jesus's answer gives a distinctively Christian motivation for fasting. And in so doing, he attributes genuine importance to it while at the same time underlining its relative character. In his response, he designates himself as the mysterious bridegroom, the anointed one who comes to establish a new alliance, and for the first time announces his death by which it will be sealed. He situates fasting, like all other religious practices, with reference to his death and rising. The faithful, after his departure, being oriented toward his return in glory, are to fast as a sign of their expectant longing for his return at the end of time. While he's here, no; but when he moves to the cross and grave, yes. Then the wedding guests will fast, and it will be their way of participating in his death and resurrection in their own bodies as they wait in hope for the day of his return.

INNER ANTICIPATORY JOY

This mystery of loving union with the bridegroom is to be marked by intimacy and discretion. In his Sermon on the Mount, Jesus insists with regard to fasting, as with regard to all other practices, not to parade them before others:

> And whenever you fast, do not look dismal, like the hypocrites, for they disfigure their faces so as to show others that they are fasting. Truly I tell you, they have received their reward. But when you fast, put oil on your head and wash your face, so that your fasting may be seen not by others but by your Father who is in secret; and your Father who sees in secret will reward you. (Matt. 6:16–18)

This teaching marks a decisive turn in the history of spiritual intentions by its emphasis on keeping a *secret* between the soul and God. Whereas before you were to wear your intention on your sleeve, now you are to hold it close to your heart discreetly. The sacrificial or "dying" aspect of it is carried inwardly while outwardly you witness with combed hair and washed face to the anticipated and joyful rising to come. As Paul, quoting Proverbs, reminds the Corinthians, "God loves a cheerful giver" (2 Cor. 9:7). So if fasting is still on the program after the bridegroom's departure, it must be renewed from within.

This renewal will necessarily involve two things: First, a discovery of the mystical and contemplative core of Christian faith (your union with the risen Lord as he is now: risen and glorified). Second, an awakening to the inner dynamism of

Christian faith as oriented to the end-time when you will have passed through the same experiences (suffering and death) to which Christ was subject in his mortality and when you will have risen with him to new life. In Paul's words: "I want to know Christ and the power of his resurrection and the sharing of his sufferings by becoming like him in his death, if somehow I may attain the resurrection from the dead" (Phil. 3:10, 11).

There's the program, and Paul states the way to realize it: "Therefore we have been buried with him by baptism into death, so that, just as Christ was raised from the dead by the glory of the Father, we too might walk in newness of life. For if we have been united with him in a death like his, we will certainly be united with him in a resurrection like his" (Rom. 6:4, 5). The renewal of the inner experience of fasting called for by Jesus can only come through embracing the mystical experience of union—already begun, but not yet fully realized—at the heart of Christian faith. Thus do the great doctors of the church, St. Augustine and St. Thomas Aquinas, speak of the "fast of exultation" inspired by the life-giving presence of the bridegroom.[1]

To recapitulate this distinctive motif in Christian fasting: Jesus's words to his followers indicate that the way in which the reign of God is rushing into the world through his presence and ministry leaves only room while he is with them for joy and thanksgiving. Jesus has come as the bridegroom to establish a mystical marriage with God's people. The time before his death was for celebrating the nuptial promises, a time for announcing the "good news": "the kingdom of God is among you" (Luke 17:21). Jesus is bringing new wine; an inner transformation is under way.

But "the days will come when the bridegroom is taken away from them, and then they will fast." Their fasting is now a recognition of something new that is already set in motion, although not yet completed: the reign of God in our midst. Henceforth, the sign of Christian fasting is to be joy and charity. After Jesus gives his life for his bride (that is, for God's people), there is an indeterminate period of waiting for his second and final coming. And during this time, his faithful are not idle, but wait with busy hands, in vigilant preparation for his return:

> You must be ready, dressed and have your lamps alight, like those who wait to welcome their lord and master on his return from the wedding feast, so that when he comes and knocks at the door, they may open it for him at once. Happy are the servants whom their lord finds on the alert when he arrives. I assure you that he will then take off his outer clothes, make them sit down to dinner, and come and wait on them. And if he should come just after midnight or in the very early morning, and find them still on the alert, their happiness is assured. (Luke 12:35–39, trans. J. B. Phillips)

Fasting is one of the ways the servants keep themselves alert in this future-oriented waiting until the bridegroom returns. To what could you liken their discreet, mysterious joy as they wait? You could say it is like the quiet humming or whistling of a choir member earlier in the day of a concert. It's like a mother and father cleaning the house and making up the beds in anticipation of the kids' coming home at Thanksgiving or Christmas. It's like standing in the airport terminal or train station, waiting for your loved one to appear. It's like a fiancée patiently addressing the wedding invitations: The long-awaited event is not here yet, but it will come, and this is necessary preparation. In each case the energy is upbeat, forward-looking, and marked by the quiet joy of anticipation.

LIBERATION THROUGH DISCIPLINE
Anyone who has ever fasted knows that there is more than simply joy in the experience! While the work of God's reign in

human hearts is at large and under way, it is not yet completed. And in the meantime, human hearts still need to become obedient and docile to the quiet work of the advocate, the Holy Spirit of God, who yearns and groans within, interceding for us with sighs too deep for words (Rom. 8:26). The human heart, scarred by weakness and sin, has difficulty in opening fully to grace, has difficulty in making God the still point at the center of frenetic and distracted lives.

Enter the penitential motif in Christian fasting, one that would perhaps be the strongest association in the minds of many. Penitence is always oriented toward freedom and liberation, although that may not always have been so clearly grasped. In Christian faith, it is not about expiating sin, for acquittal has already been granted. The tendency is to think that God will love us if we change, but God loves us so that we *can* change. Penitential practices and disciplines enable us to appropriate and make real in our lives the freedom given through grace. They help readjust priorities and remind where real treasure lies. Jesus's own going into the desert for forty days tells us that there will be little control or moderation unless there is also something of dying—dying to those areas of our lives where we are *too* alive, where egotism and self-concern block discernment of what God may be asking and create resistance to conforming our own wills to the will of God because of what it will cost. Jesus prepared himself by fasting for what lay ahead of him, and his example instructs at least as much as his words.

To the early church fell the challenge of finding the balance between the inner conviction of the gift given and the undeniable reality in daily living of a gift not yet fully awakened to, received, and given sway in thoughts, words, and actions. The man who saw the way forward and blazed the trail was Paul. It is sometimes said that Jesus came preaching the kingdom of God but that it was Paul who laid the foundation for the growth and development of the church. One-third of what is called the New

Testament are his letters, and the letter to the Thessalonians is the oldest document in the New Testament. Paul's great theme is freedom: "For you were called to freedom, brothers and sisters, only do not use your freedom for self-indulgence but through love become servants to one another" (Gal. 5:13).

It is Paul's deepest desire that the followers of the new way benefit from the practices of the spiritual life as *means* without becoming enslaved to them. "In every circumstance and in all things I have learned the secret of being well-fed and of going hungry, of having plenty and being in need. I can do all things through him who strengthens me" (Phil. 4:12–13). Paul gives no interdictions regarding food any religious significance:

I know and am persuaded in the Lord Jesus that nothing is unclean in itself; but it is unclean for anyone who thinks it is unclean. (Rom. 14:14)

Eat whatever is sold in the meat market without raising any question on the ground of conscience, for the earth and the fullness thereof are the Lord's. (1 Cor. 10:25–26)

Therefore do not let anyone condemn you in matters of food and drink.... Why do you submit to regulations, "Do not handle, Do not taste, Do not touch"? All these regulations refer to simply human commands and teachings ... but they are of no value in checking self-indulgence. (Col. 2:16, 20–23)

At the same time, Paul witnesses to fasts of his own (2 Cor. 6:4–5; 11:27) and clearly recognizes the place of discipline and voluntary self-privation:

Athletes exercise self-control in all things: they do it to receive a perishable wreath, but we an imperishable one.

So I do not run aimlessly, nor do I box as though beating the air; but I punish my body and enslave it, so that after proclaiming to others I myself should not be disqualified. (1 Cor. 9:25–27)

Paul has staked out the terrain, and the evolving tradition of Christian asceticism begins to work with it. *Ascetical* comes from the Greek *askesis,* which means "exercise, training, discipline." Accordingly, ascetical life is either the whole project of appropriating the divine gift of grace or, more frequently, the work of purification. Ascetical practices are methods designed to restrain the influence of sin and maximize union with God. The whole work goes forward under the influence of grace (the Holy Spirit)—the mystical element of Christian life. Christian life is radically and ultimately mystical, but the mystical union is received and fostered in the personal engagement and struggle of asceticism. Ascetical practices, of which fasting is one, are human strategies for spiritual living.[2]

The laboratory in which ascetical practices took root, grew, and were widely imitated was the Christian monastic tradition. The entire tradition of monasticism bears witness that union with God is the highest state of consciousness and usually presupposes a life of self-discipline rather than a life of self-indulgence. Everything comes with a price tag on it; a strong love is willing to pay the price. The human price tag on the contemplative experience of God is persevering self-discipline, except in cases of extraordinary divine intervention. The normal path is that pointed out by Jesus: "If any want to become my followers, let them deny themselves and take up their cross and follow me" (Matt. 16:24). Cistercian monk Charles Cummings offers his perception of how we become liberated through discipline:

The more I try to make Christ the center of my life and thoughts and actions, the more I feel every pull and tug that draws me back from the radical, loving surrender of myself. I am not totally free to run toward the one I love. Instead, I feel enchained, entangled by a thousand little threads that together form a strong rope binding me to myself. Detaching myself from these bonds is largely a matter of self-discipline and asceticism. Paradoxically, self-discipline sets me free for God. Self-discipline is a training in freedom. I am free to take something comfortable and pleasurable, or to eat and drink more, or to sleep longer, but I am also free to refrain from these things and not let myself be held bound by them. True Christian freedom is the freedom of those who live no longer for themselves, the freedom of being a new creation in Christ (2 Cor. 5:15, 17). The movement of self-discipline leads out of bondage to the self into an experience of newness and freedom, then back again to a liberated use and appreciation and enjoyment of material goods, in moderation, without becoming entangled again by a thousand little threads....

Monastic self-discipline is a subtle technique of liberation, proceeding with firmness but not with a heavy-handed repression that would try to extinguish human feelings and emotions or to refuse all use of material goods. Nor does self-discipline fall to the seduction of body culture, instead it attunes the whole self to hear the deeper calls and values of life in Christ. The word "discipline," from *discere* (Latin, "to learn"), suggests an attitude of listening and learning, an attitude of discipleship. I put my whole self into the school of the Lord's service and become a listener to the voice of the Spirit within me. And where the Spirit of the Lord is, there is freedom (2 Cor. 3:17). The Spirit always calls us to move beyond ourselves in loving response to others. At first it may seem that the requirements of spiritual excellence destroy freedom, but in fact they are in the service of true freedom. This principle holds true in every field of excellence. Time and persistent self-imposed discipline are the key to a mastery that can be creatively free. Dance instructor Martha Graham has said of her art: "Your goal is freedom, but freedom may only be achieved through discipline. In the studio you learn to conform, to submit yourself to the demands of your craft so that you may finally be free."[3]

In recent years, Cummings notes, there has been a decreased tendency to impose fasting on the entire monastic community, though some communities may, by consensus, designate a particular day on a regular basis as a day of fasting. But more and more the degree and frequency of fasting is left to the responsible judgment of each individual. The one who comes to it is then not only ready and willing, but lively and in high spirits. Practices that are shouldered reluctantly, with gloomy looks and groans, probably do not touch the deep root of desire, while those that are offered to God with a sincerely joyful heart and a cheerful countenance are likely to be more fruitful and effective. He is careful to note that even though we speak of *self*-discipline, spiritual liberation and transformation are always a gift of grace.[4]

His testimony clearly shows that Christian asceticism is not antihuman or antibody or antiworld, though these qualities have sometimes surfaced in history. The primary reason for asceticism is the call to liberation from the "thousand little threads that make a rope" and bind us, the call to become free for service in love.

WORK OF CHARITY AND JUSTICE

Jesus remained entirely faithful to the traditional triad of practices that were his Jewish heritage and that we have already seen in the previous chapter: prayer, fasting, and almsgiving. So much so, that a whole section of his Sermon on the Mount (Matt. 6:1–18) is structured according to that schema, except that he changes the order to almsgiving, prayer, and fasting. We have already cited above his teaching on "when you fast," but not the preceding verses, which provide a catechesis on almsgiving and prayer:

> Beware of practicing your piety before others in order to be seen by them; for then you have no reward from your Father in heaven.
>
> So whenever you give alms, do not sound a trumpet before you, as the hypocrites do in the synagogues and in the streets, so that they may be praised by others. Truly I tell you, they have received their reward. But when you give alms, do not let your left hand know what your right hand is doing, so that your alms may be done in secret; and your Father who sees in secret will reward you.
>
> And whenever you pray, do not be like the hypocrites; for they love to stand and pray in the synagogues and at the street corners, so that they may be seen by others. Truly I tell you, they have received their reward. But whenever you pray, go into your room and shut the door and pray to your Father who is in secret; and your Father who sees in secret will reward you.
>
> When you are praying, do not heap up empty phrases as the Gentiles do; for they think that they will be heard because of their many words. Do not be like them, for your Father knows what you need before you ask him. (Matt. 6:1–8)

And then follows the teaching about not looking gloomy when you fast, but washing your face and combing your hair so that you may not appear to be fasting, except to your Father in heaven who is hidden (Matt. 6:16–18). Consistent with the

Jewish ideal of fasting, Jesus underlines the essential quality of humility, a message he reiterates in the parable of the publican and the Pharisee, whose practice of fasting fails to justify him because of his pride and disdain for the publican (Luke 18:9–14).

In contrast to John the Baptist and his disciples, Jesus and his followers do not fast. They feast, rather, as a sign of the banquet in the kingdom of God at which the poor and the marginalized are the guests of honor. Sharing bread as a sign of solidarity with the disadvantaged is more important to Jesus than fasting.

The relationship between fasting and almsgiving is a prominent theme in patristic literature. The *Shepherd of Hermas* reads: "In the day on which you fast you will taste nothing but bread and water; and having reckoned up the price of the dishes of that day which you intended to have eaten, you will give it to a widow, or an orphan, or to some person in want, and thus you will exhibit humility of mind, so that the one who has received benefit from your humility may fill his own soul" (Similitude III 5:3). For St. John Chrysostom (circa 329–407 CE), courageous bishop of Constantinople and reputed to be the greatest preacher in Greek, fasting without almsgiving was not fasting at all (*Homilies on Matthew* 77.6). The literarily prodigious Eastern Father Origen (circa 185–254 CE) blessed those who fasted in order "to nourish the poor" (*Homilies on Leviticus* 10.2). For St. Augustine (354–430 CE), who holds preeminence among the Western fathers, fasting was merely avarice unless one gave away what one would have eaten (*Sermon* 208). Whatever kind of fasting it was, in order to elevate the soul, it had to have two wings: prayer and works of mercy (*Sermon* 206). Elsewhere, he altered the image, saying that almsgiving and fasting are the wings of prayer:

> Break your bread for those who are hungry, said Isaiah,
> do not believe that fasting suffices. Fasting chastises you,

but it does not refresh the other. Your privations shall bear fruit if you give generously to another.... Do you wish your prayer to reach God? Give it two wings, fasting and almsgiving. (discourse on Ps. 42, section 8)

And to the Epicurean dictum mentioned by Paul, "Eat and drink, for tomorrow we die" (1 Cor. 15:32), St. Augustine composed a rejoinder: "Fast, pray, and give, for tomorrow we die." Then, noting that it was not an exact parallelism because there was an imbalance between the two, he adds: If one wishes to have only two terms—since the Epicurean formula has only two—it is worth more to pray and give than to fast and omit the giving (*Sermon* 150).

St. John Cassian (circa 360–435 CE), whose *Conferences* and *Institutes* exerted a far-reaching influence in Western monasticism, recounted how the desert fathers would not only break their fast if a visitor came to see them, but they would give the visitor the food they were planning on eating once their fast was over. It was their way of showing mercy, which causes Cassian to say that all the virtues of which Isaiah 58 speaks—mercy, patience, charity—should never be subordinated to fasting; on the contrary, it is fasting that is subordinate to them and serves only to advance one in those virtues. It is always the instrument and never the goal. The mortification of the flesh and the rigors of abstinence, he writes, are only means to arrive at charity and love (*Conference* 21).

The great Franciscan teacher St. Bonaventure (circa 1217–1274 CE) has his own variation on the same theme. He orders the triad thus: prayer, almsgiving, and fasting. He links prayer to the contemplative dimension of Christian life, almsgiving to the active dimension, and casts fasting in the role of supporting both. There is a notable teaching here: To dispose ourselves to contemplation, the pathway is prayer. To develop the moral virtues, the most efficacious way is the sharing of what we have with the needy. Fasting supports us in doing both.[5]

St. Peter Chrysologos (circa 450 CE), archbishop of Ravenna and doctor of the church, described the relationship of fasting to almsgiving in poetic terms: Mercy and almsgiving are to fasting what spring is to the earth: It makes the field flower (*Sermon* 8). Charitable giving is to fasting what the seed is to the field: Without it, it bears no fruit (*Sermon* 42). Or yet again: Throw the seed of your fast into the eyes of the poor, for the virtues of fasting dry up if they are not irrigated by the cries of the destitute (*Sermon* 43).

The preaching of the church fathers and later teachers clearly understands that whatever savings is realized through fasting belongs to the poor. Thus St. Gregory the Great, bishop of Rome, preached that those who do not give to the poor what they have saved but keep it for later to satisfy their own appetite do not fast for God.[6] And to those who couldn't fast, for whatever reason, and therefore had saved nothing to give to the poor, St. Augustine had this counsel: Give even more generously, because if you haven't been able to intensify your supplications with fasting, entrust a generous offering to the poor and your gift will know how to pray effectively for you before God (*Sermon* 209).

St. Leo the Great, who served as pope from 440 to 461 CE, repeatedly stressed almsgiving and other social aspects of Christian life:

> We enjoin on you this fast and urge you to practice not only abstinence from nourishment but also the works of mercy, so that you may transform into food for the poor that which you have removed from your ordinary table by religious sobriety. (*Sermon* 189)

Many more examples could be given of this theme in the history of Christian spiritual practice, but these should suffice to adequately demonstrate the unbreakable linkage between fasting and works of mercy in Christian preaching and teaching. It strengthens the desire to help the poor by restructuring the distribution of material goods and teaches one to use the earth's resources with care and respect.

In contemporary theological reflection, this emphasis is placed more on justice than acts of charity. There is a long tradition of fasting in approaching the Lord's Supper or Eucharist. The most comprehensive theological forum in Christendom, the Faith and Order Commission of the World Council of Churches, spelled out clearly for Christians the implications of their participation at the table:

> The Eucharistic celebration demands reconciliation and sharing among all those regarded as brothers and sisters in the one family of God and is a constant challenge in the search for appropriate relationships in social, economic and political life (Matt. 5:23ff; 1 Cor. 10:16ff; 1 Cor. 11:20–22; Gal. 3:28). All kinds of injustice, racism, separation and lack of freedom are radically challenged when we share in the body and blood of Christ.... As participants in the Eucharist, therefore, we prove inconsistent if we are not actively participating in this ongoing restoration of the world's situation and the human condition. The Eucharist shows us that our behavior is inconsistent in the face of the reconciling presence of God in human history: we are placed under continual judgment by the persistence of unjust relationships of all kinds in our society, the manifold divisions on account of human pride, material interest and power politics and, above all, the obstinacy of unjustifiable confessional oppositions within the body of Christ.

> Solidarity in the Eucharistic communion of the body of Christ and responsible care of Christians for one another and for the world find specific expression in the

liturgies: in the mutual forgiveness of sins; the sign of peace; intercession for all; the eating and drinking together; the taking of the elements to the sick and those in prison or the celebration of the Eucharist with them. All these manifestations of love in the Eucharist are directly related to Christ's own testimony as a servant, in whose servanthood Christians themselves participate.[7]

The World Council of Churches' declaration of a decade (2001–2010) to overcome violence provides another example of how churches today are working creatively with the practice of fasting in its traditional triadic framework of prayer, fasting, and almsgiving. In conjunction with the decade, U.S. member churches of the World Council of Churches are calling annually for a Lenten fast from violence. The invitation is for all Christians to *pray* regularly the Peace Prayer attributed to St. Francis of Assisi ("Lord, make me an instrument of your peace"); to examine your life and choose a *fast* that has personal and/or communal meaning, for example, fast from violent TV shows, movies, video games, from products manufactured in sweatshops or by child labor, from financial investment in companies that produce violence; and to *give* over and above your regular offerings to support the work of programs that address the causes of violence, alleviate its consequences, or that work for peace and reconciliation.[8]

We have looked at three major motifs in the history of the Christian practice of fasting. How did these motivating themes take concrete expression in the life of the early church and with what form and frequency?

FASTING IN THE EARLY CHRISTIAN CHURCH

The primitive church took over the custom of fasting from Judaism, from which comes the oldest injunction we have concerning Christian fasting, that is, two days per week were designated as fast days. The Jews observed Monday and Thursday, and whoever wished to fast did so on those two days, although there was no general command to fast. The gentile Christian churches appointed Wednesday and Friday.

As we have seen, Jesus established no specific legislation on fasting but left it to the church to determine, underlining the critical importance of renewing the practice from within. During the time of his letters to young Christian churches (thirty to fifty years after Jesus's death and resurrection), Paul offered his own example of voluntary fasts to encourage others, but for Paul the key concept is freedom and liberty in the Spirit. We must first of all grasp the profound reality that the divine life-giving Spirit of God has been given freely, as a gift, and dwells within. Through this inner, mystical union with the risen Christ through the Holy Spirit, fasting and praying and sharing our goods with the poor comes from a place of deep gratitude and is to be done with an inner quiet joy and peace and serenity.

There is very little in the Acts of the Apostles that witnesses with any detail to the community's practice of fasting; one is left with a sense of great diversity and freedom in the Spirit. At the same time, we are given glimpses of the interwoven association of prayer and fasting. Before Paul and Barnabas set off on a special mission to bring the good news of Jesus Christ to others, the prophets and teachers and whole community fasted and prayed, "then after fasting and praying they laid their hands on them and sent them off" (Acts 13:2–3; 14:23).

The early Christian writers—Justin, Polycarp, Hermas, Pseudo-Barnabas—constantly exhorted their readers to fast. The earliest source books, like the *Didache,* the *Canons of the Apostolic Didascalias,* and the *Apostolic Constitutions,* preserve for us a record of what was going on among the earliest Christian communities. In the discussion of the third theme above, we saw several examples of the most notable preachers of the era encouraging the faithful to fast and to give what they had saved to the poor. In his

Apology, Aristides, a journalist, explained to Emperor Hadrian in about 128 CE the manner in which the Christians lived: "When someone is poor among them who has need of help, they fast for two or three days, and they have the custom of sending him the food which they had prepared for themselves" (15, 9).

The Lord's Supper was to be received fasting as well. Out of such practices, the fast before Easter developed. Easter is the only annual festival of the church going back to the first century, and the gradual appointment of a general fast beforehand was only to observe a custom that was everywhere considered a matter of course. The first clear evidence of this custom turns up in the second century, where we find the day before Easter as a fast day in one place, the two or more days before Easter in another place, and the custom of fasting for forty hours before the Easter celebration in yet another place. In general, the idea was to make the duration of the fast coextensive with the amount of time Christ spent in the tomb.

At Easter, new members were received into the worshiping community through baptism. In a fitting example of encouragement with flexibility and freedom, the *Didache* prescribes that both the baptizer and the baptized, and others who are able, fast for one or two days prior (7, 4). It is also instructive to see that the repentance and conversion called for by entry into the "new life" are accompanied by prayer and fasting.

In the course of the third century, the fast was extended to the six days of Holy Week. The innovation was combined with the already established custom of fasting a day or two before Easter by making the fast on the last two days—Good Friday and Holy Saturday—more strict. Here we see again the theme of mystical union: The faithful identify themselves with the Lord in his suffering, reproducing an experience of "dying" in their own bodies that they may also know the power of his resurrection in their bodies on the last day. The commemoration of the death of Jesus on Friday is very old, and it is possible that from the beginning, the death of Jesus was commemorated every Friday, just as his resurrection was celebrated every Sunday.

Another third-century development in Rome was the establishment of a third weekly fast day, Saturday (in addition to Wednesday and Friday). The Saturday fast was considered a weekly repetition of the fast before Easter. This Roman innovation, however, did not spread widely. The Eastern Christian churches always declined to adopt it. When in the West three fast days per week appeared too many, it was Wednesday, not Friday or Saturday, that was given up.

At the beginning of the fourth century, in the time of a great persecution of Christians, the forty-day fast was introduced on the analogy of the forty-day fast of Jesus in the desert, and Lent was born. The custom of different churches varied in the fourth century, but by the fifth century, a certain amount of harmony was reached by fixing the fast at either six or seven weeks. Rome observed six, the Eastern churches seven, and this is the present custom of the Western and Eastern churches respectively.

From the middle of the fourth century, the birth of Jesus was celebrated on December 25, and it struck the people as natural that, like Easter, the new high festival also should be preceded by a forty-day fast. Rome, a moderating influence even then, reduced the original time to the present four weeks of Advent.

Just how seriously did the people take all these fasting days? The requirement of fasting during the whole of Lent and Advent proved too difficult, especially for the segment of the population that rarely had regular mealtimes and were accustomed to only meager and primitive food. Already in the fourth century, during the lifetime of people who had themselves witnessed the implementation of these customs, a consensus emerged that they would fast two or three weeks but not the whole forty days.

Fasting was generally understood as abstinence from all food until evening, or one meal a day, which was to be as simple as possible. In the first century, that translated into bread, salt, and water. Later on, fruits and eggs, sometimes fish, and even poultry were allowed, so that the fasting was finally limited to the prohibition of red meat and wine. To limit thus the enjoyment of food to the barest necessities, or to refrain from certain designated kinds of food, constituted "abstinence" in the technical sense.

The increasing effort to structure the fasting experience within this or that fixed time, and to make distinctions between fasting and abstinence, is particularly understandable given the communitarian dimension of the observance. Nevertheless, it represents an entry onto a slippery slope whereon one increasingly risks approaching the practice in a legalistic way. Every religion struggles with the challenge of keeping the means from becoming ends in their ascetical practices.

What is the situation today, and what inspiration and guidance might contemporary Christians draw for their lives from these motifs and their concrete expression in historically institutionalized forms?

THE SITUATION TODAY

In the Anglican and mainline Protestant churches today, the question of fasting is left to the individual member. Each decides for him- or herself whether to fast and how. In the Anglican Communion, the more important fast days are recommended in the Book of Common Prayer. The list includes all Fridays, Lent, the Ember Days (seasonal observances of penance, thanksgiving, and petition for divine blessing occurring on a Wednesday, Friday, and Saturday four times a year), and certain vigils, but it merely enjoins a special measure of devotion and abstinence on these days. No precise laws are given, such details being left to the discretion of local ecclesiastical authorities.

For Evangelical Christians, fasting is generally linked with intercessory prayer. There is a sense that if one is really serious about something, one does not just pray, but rather chooses to "fast and pray." Few Evangelicals have fasting as a regular spiritual practice, even though it was very much part of the spiritual disciplines of John Wesley. Usually fasting is practiced occasionally, in response to a particular need, for which "we will fast and pray." It is also usually something that is done as a group, for example, in all-night prayer meetings or when members "skip lunch" to spend time in intercessory prayer.

Lutherans in some quarters are taking active interest in making relevant for contemporary practice Martin Luther's positive recommendation: "Of fasting I say this: it is right to fast frequently in order to subdue and control the body."[9] In his *Small Catechism,* Luther also commended fasting as a fitting preparation for receiving Holy Communion. What this highlights is a cultic asceticism that has been found not only in Christianity but in all formal religions. Cultic asceticism touches on abstinence and acts preparatory to participation in the mysteries of divine cult and liturgy. In the Hebrew scriptures there are various examples of this expressed in fasting, vigils, sexual abstinence, washings, and the offering of incense and of animals.

It is in the Eastern Church that we find the cultic asceticism of fasting more in evidence than anywhere. Days observed by fasting and abstinence have been so numerous at different times that the total has been as high as 180 days in the course of a year. And all of them come as preparatory acts for participation in the liturgical mysteries. In addition to the great, or major, Lent, three other "Lents" have been observed in the Greek Church: the Lent of the Holy Apostles (June 16–28), Mary's Lent (August 1–14), and the Lent preceding Christmas (November 15–December 24). Fasting was also observed, besides these four extended seasons, on the vigils of the Epiphany, St. John the Baptist's Day, Holy Cross Day, and every Wednesday and Friday. Today, much of such cultic preparation has been relegated to individual inspiration, and the church members as a whole do not generally enter into any common cultic preparation in such an ascetical manner.

The literature on fasting among Orthodox Christians emphasizes that at all times it is essential to bear in mind "that sin will have no dominion over you, since you are not under law but under grace" (Rom. 6:14) and that "the letter kills but the spirit gives life" (2 Cor. 3:6). The rules of fasting apply to dairy, meat, wine, and olive oil; while they need to be taken seriously, these rules are not to be interpreted with dour and pedantic legalism, "for the kingdom of God is not food and drink, but righteousness and peace and joy in the Holy Spirit" (Rom. 14:17).

Pope Paul VI sought to renew "penitential discipline with practices more suited to our times" with the apostolic constitution *Poenitemini* (February 17, 1966). Insisting upon the preeminently interior and religious character of penitence, the pope warns that true penance cannot ever "prescind from physical asceticism as well." He notes that the fundamental means of fulfilling the divine precept of penance is through prayer, fasting, and charity. In November 1966, the U.S. Catholic Bishops issued a Pastoral Statement on Penance and Abstinence, which remains a source of inspiration and guidance for all Christians:

> Christ died for our salvation on Friday. Gratefully remembering this, Catholic peoples from time immemorial have set apart Friday for special penitential observance by which they gladly suffer with Christ that they may one day be glorified with him.... Since the spirit of penance primarily suggests that we discipline ourselves in that which we enjoy most, to many in our day abstinence from meat no longer implies penance, while renunciation of other things would be more penitential.
>
> For these and related reasons, the Catholic bishops of the United States, far from downgrading the traditional penitential observance of Friday, and motivated

precisely by the desire to give the spirit of penance greater vitality, especially on Fridays, the day that Jesus died, urge our Catholic people henceforth to be guided by the following norms.

Friday itself remains a special day of penitential observance throughout the year.... Friday should be in each week something of what Lent is in the entire year. For this reason we urge all to prepare for that weekly Easter that comes with each Sunday by freely making of every Friday a day of self-denial and mortification in prayerful remembrance of the passion of Jesus Christ.

Among the works of voluntary self-denial and personal penance which we especially recommend to our people ... we give first place to abstinence from flesh meat. We do so in the hope that the Catholic community will ordinarily continue to abstain from meat by free choice as formerly we did in obedience to Church law.... Our deliberate, personal abstinence from meat, more especially because no longer required by law, will be an outward sign of inward spiritual values that we cherish....

Fridays, please God, will acquire among us other forms of penitential witness which may become as much a part of the devout way of life in the future as Friday abstinence from meat.... It would bring great glory to God and good to souls if Fridays found our people doing volunteer work in hospitals, visiting the sick, serving the needs of the aged and the lonely, instructing the young in the faith, participating as Christians in community affairs, and meeting our obligations to our families, our friends, our neighbors, and our communities, including our parishes, with a special zeal ... born of living faith....

Let it be proved by the spirit in which we enter upon prayer and penance, not excluding fast and abstinence freely chosen, that these present decisions and recommendations of this conference of bishops will herald a new birth of loving faith and a more profound penitential conversion, by both of which we become one with Christ, mature sons and daughters of God, and servants of God's people.[10]

The Canadian Conference of Catholic Bishops' liturgical office reiterated the new approach in 1986:

Throughout the year, every Friday is a day of abstinence from meat, obliging all Catholics who are 14 or older. We may substitute special *acts of charity* (such as visiting the sick or aged, helping those in any need, or contributing time or money to a work of charity) or *acts of piety* (taking part in a service of worship with others, praying with our family, or spending some time in personal prayer, especially with God's holy word in the scriptures).[11]

What these communications make clear is that spiritual exercises and devotional practices don't exist for themselves. They exist to help us express and grow in our faith, our hope, our love, our gratitude. They exist to help us become more genuinely open to the acceptance of God's will, to assist us in looking upon the events of our lives with faith, and to enable us to make ourselves more and more aware of God as the deepest reality of our lives. The value of any particular practice is related to its ability or effectiveness in doing that. When we have lost the spirit of the practice and are engaged largely in a repetition of its form, it is perhaps better that it is lost for a time so that it can be rediscovered again and embraced once more—freely, with understanding and positive desire.

There are many factors that contributed to the revamping of the approach to fasting in the Catholic Church. To cite but several:

- A dualistic conception of the body and soul that resulted in fasting being seen as the combat of the spirit
  against the body
- A reduction in a scientific era of what is real to what
  can be rationally explained and empirically verified; the
  loss of a sense of the interpenetration of the spiritual
  and the sensate
- A juridical approach that gradually smothers the mystical spirit at the origin of the practice
- The erosion of personal and communal faith in an
  increasingly secular society
- An intellectualization of faith incapable of supporting
  practices like fasting and prayer, which flow from deep
  dispositions of the heart ("to believe" comes from the Latin
  credere, the root of which is *cor dare,* "to give one's heart")
- The overturning of traditional customs, mental frameworks, and life rhythms in a technological society
- Instability and complexity as new modes of life[12]

I think it would be fair to say that Christians in general
today have largely lost the sense of fasting, no longer know how
or why or when, and are at a loss as to how to meaningfully
reconnect with the tradition. But if our present circumstance is
the occasion for rediscovering treasure tried and true, reappro-
priating it, and integrating it into our living with new appreciation for its value, then there is a hidden grace in the moment.

RECLAIMING THE BEST ELEMENTS FROM THE TRADITION

The Christian church must in every age interpret the old truths
in new, fresh forms. An enlightened contemporary spirituality
attempts to keep continuity with the past but also to relate the
explosion of knowledge in the human and sacred sciences to a viable
practice. In our age, the climate of spirituality is incarnational,

not apocalyptic or excessively turned toward the end-time. It is the goodness of creation that is emphasized, rather than the transitory quality of life or the pervasive presence of sin. A healthy contemporary Christian asceticism will not attack or deny what has already been redeemed.

Today's asceticism is holistic and looks to total human development, the interpenetration of the human and the Divine. It comes out of life's circumstances, is less prepackaged and more the response of love. The goal is the integration of all life, personal and social, in Christ. The old language of denial and mortification is unpopular today because in the present context people are more inclined to embrace spiritual life practices for their liberating, life-giving potential, rather than for punishing the body or compensating for guilt. Ascetical practices today search especially for growth in human authenticity and the achievement of human community, especially through the promotion of justice and peace. Such a this-worldly spirituality does well to follow the balanced formula of our Jewish roots and of the early church, which saw the core of its life expressed in prayer, fasting, and almsgiving.[13]

A LIVING VOICE FROM THE TRADITION

The "living voice from the tradition" in this chapter will be my own. Allow me, then, in this closing section to speak not with the at-arm's-length air of the observer and reporter, but with the subjective voice of a participant who stands within the tradition and who has been for the past thirty years a student and practitioner of its accumulated wisdom on fasting. Rather than spending more time describing the present situation, I would prefer to identify some characteristics that I hope would mark a renaissance of this valuable spiritual life practice among Christians today.

Fasting is freely embraced out of a personally perceived value. The point at which our human freedom reaches its peak is when we, having experienced in our daily lives the abundant love of God for us, move freely, spontaneously, and with a spirit of improvisation to return God's love. Thus we may freely offer to God a day's fasting or work in a homeless shelter out of a sheer desire to love God. Such a motive represents the quintessential religious act: a desire to return love by love.

Its two "wings" are prayer and almsgiving. The triadic formula sums up the Christian vocation in key symbolic acts that express the triple relationship to God, self, and others. The "wings" approach at one and the same time deepens our relationship with Christ and strengthens the community. There is no coaching on techniques for practices like fasting or meditation in the letters of Paul. For him, the virtues that matter are those that build up community: forgiveness, mercy, cooperation, patience, love.

It is sensitive to and follows the Spirit's lead. Fundamentally, fasting represents offering ourselves to God in a spirit of openness and readiness, inviting the action of the Holy Spirit. Such an impulse comes from God and is not of our own planning. The movement of the Spirit within is important so that fasting may be a true, religious act of loving worship and self-surrender. This means that it will always be more than a technique taken on solely for health purposes or expanded consciousness. Fasting as a response to God's initiative results in practical outreach. We will respond to the need we see; the fast God has chosen prepares us within in such a way that we can be used to bring about change in outward circumstances.

It is not just for Lent but for Christian life. If prayer, fasting, and works of justice form the core of Christian life and are inextricably linked, how can any one of them remain quarantined to just one season of the liturgical year? They are all essential elements of Christian living *throughout* the year.

Fasting accords priority to that day in the week when Jesus revealed God's immeasurable love for us: Friday. The ways of responding to the wonder of a love are many; a valuable point of reference is the pattern in the early centuries. Fasting was generally understood as abstinence of all food until evening, or one meal a day, which was to be as simple as possible.

It finds meaningful expression in preparation for receiving the Eucharist. When something or someone greater is coming our way, we're generally willing to put the eating on hold. Forgoing whatever meal precedes Sunday worship creates a psychic as well as a physical space within to receive Christ who comes to fill us with his hunger and his thirst. It is an instance where mystical joy and anticipation spring up at the anticipated encounter with the risen one.

Its approach is holistic. Spiritual growth is the slow work of God's grace helping us to fully accept and harmoniously integrate all the dimensions of our selves. We are not body *and* soul (two things); we are enspirited flesh: one reality. When we embrace that incredibly rich and exciting reality and love it, we are accepting and appreciating the self God has given us in all its totality.

Its characteristic virtue is humility. We are created from nothing, and what God wants us to bring is our nothingness, our creatureliness, our recognition that we are always and everywhere utterly dependent on our Creator for all good things.

It is marked by moderation. Like everything else in the spiritual life, it's not about doing it all or doing it right; it's just about doing it in a spirit of faith and love. There is no "ladder theology" here of earning our way on the performance principle. Our doing does not create our being. Our being "in Christ" is a gift. In religious language, we're justified not by works but by faith in God's love.

It often has traces of quiet joy within it. Since God is our well-being, when we are rightly focused on God, all else falls into perspective. The balanced life that flows naturally from this perspective is a path of deep, peaceful serenity that comes from being rooted in a solid place. It is only when fasting is seen as a focus on God as our rock, our fortress, our shelter in time of stress that we can understand why fasting is characterized by quiet joy.

It stays close to its mystical inspiration. For so many, Christianity is a moral matter, whereas in fact it's a mystical matter. "Mystical" here refers to our participation in the very life of God by our being "in Christ." When we get the relationship part right, the moral living follows naturally behind.

It is a flexible instrument of the spiritual life that can be worked with creatively. Unity in the spirit with a lot of diversity in its realizations has characterized the life of the church in its brightest and healthiest eras. The choice is between a variety of realizations united in spirit or a conformity without spirit that is a sin against and extinguishes the Holy Spirit. (At the end of chapter 9, several "nontraditional" ways of working with the dynamics of fasting are given.)

Always when we voluntarily go without food, it's because something else is more important to us. It might be skipping breakfast to leave the house early or dieting to achieve a slim waistline or physical well-being. But when it's done as a religious act in the Christian tradition, at the heart of it is this: God, you are number one for me;

you are more important than life itself, which food sym-
bolizes for me. The fast brings home to me in a real and
concrete way that God is the essential source of all life and
well-being. The focus away from food (and what it sym-
bolizes as one of the goods of existence that we need) to
God is deliberate. Yes, these other goods are important.
Yes, I need them. But all the needs in my life, if traced
down to their deepest core, are rooted in my single, greatest need: for fulfillment from the hand of my Creator.

During times of fasting, the simple fact that we're
not walking out of the shop or office or living room
toward the refrigerator or restaurant, the simple sensations emitted by an empty stomach, will serve to remind
us of God's presence in our lives, because it was for this
that we deliberately determined to disrupt our routine
today. Meals *are* important in so many ways—as a social
event, as a needed break from work, as nutrition—and
when we voluntarily forgo this, as part of the language of
our relationship with God, it takes on the meaning that
we are willing to set aside all else that would interfere with
seeking God wholeheartedly. By setting aside what sym-
bolizes life and growth to tend to our relationship with
God, we are declaring that God is more important and
essential a source of life and growth than anything else.

From time to time we forget just which needs are
the most important, and our priorities become confused.
Fasting cuts through the drift and ambiguity like a meat
cleaver coming down on a butcher's table. It is a concrete,
decisive act that says, "You, Lord, are the still point in my
turning world, and please don't let me ever forget it. For
you, I will upset my routine today of three meals because
you are the God I worship, not my work or routine
(which becomes all too important for me sometimes). For
you I will give up meeting my friends for lunch today

because, even though I need them and like them very much, the love and acceptance I need from them is only a reflection of the love and acceptance I need from you. For you I will live with these hunger pangs today and let them speak to me of my deepest hungers. Our hearts are restless, Lord, until they rest in you."

It has been the constant experience of men and women who fast that abstaining from food not only frees them to focus on God with fresh intensity, but opens avenues of spiritual perception and understanding that are not available during the rush of routine living. They find a clarity of direction and quickening of spirit as they focus on God with intentionality. Fasting itself is not the power—God is. When our hearts are freed from debris and clutter, the Holy Spirit can flow through us more freely. We become clearer witnesses to God's presence and action in the world.

CHAPTER FOUR

ISLAM:
ALLAH-CONSCIOUSNESS,
SELF-RESTRAINT, SOCIAL
SOLIDARITY

Islam aims to transform the whole of human life into a life of worship. We are born servants, and to serve the Creator is our very nature. To surrender to Allah in thought, word, and deed, to obey and submit to Allah's will, to remain conscious always and everywhere of what we ought to do or to avoid to earn the pleasure of Allah: This is living a life of worship.

One of the acts of worship that Allah enjoins upon Muslims is *sawm,* or fasting. It means abstaining from eating, drinking, and sexual relations from dawn to sunset. Fasting is the third of the five pillars or religious obligations in Islam. The most concentrated time of fasting for Muslims is the ninth month on the Islamic calendar, Ramadan. For over one billion Muslims throughout the world and eight million in North America, it is a time of inner reflection, cultivation of Allah-consciousness, and self-control. Muslims think of it as a time of spiritual tune-up in the year. The month of fasting in Islam is a month of worship welcomed with energy and happiness. As it is one of the five pillars of Islam, any failure to observe it without reasonable excuse is a grave sin in the sight of God.

How and why did this practice get started? God commanded it. In the Qur'an (2:185), we read:

> The month of Ramadan, in which was revealed the Qur'an, a guide to mankind, with explanations for direction and discernment. Whoever of you is in a position to do so, let him fast the month, and whoever is ill or on a journey (fast) the same number of other days. Allah desires ease for you, He does not desire hardship for you: and that you should complete the time appointed, and that you should glorify Allah for giving you this guidance, that you may be thankful.

Some scholars see a direct link with fasting practice in the Hebrew and Christian scriptures. The forty-day fasts of Moses (Exod. 34:28), Elijah (1 Kings 19:8), and Jesus (Matt. 4:2) indicate that biblical fasting is not partial but complete, that is, nothing can be eaten or drunk. The great length of these fasts indicates that, since it is stated to be a complete fast, some eating and drinking during the night must have been permitted. Also, it is noted that, to placate the Lord, the prophet Jeremiah proclaimed a fast in the ninth month for all the people of Jerusalem and the cities of Judah (Jer. 36:3–7). Further, Isaiah 58 clearly describes the kind of fast God wants: There are some other pleasures besides food and drink that are to be abstained from, and the fast must be marked by compassion for the hunger of the poor and doing something to alleviate it. In summary, biblical fasting serves as another affirmative point of reference: It is seen as complete abstention from eating, drinking, and some other pleasures during the daylight hours of the lunar calendar, and it includes acts of charity and justice.[1] These biblical passages also indicate to Muslims that fasting is not new and that it was prescribed to those before them. They are not the only ones requested to fast; if there is variation in its practice among those who believe in the God of Abraham, it is due to the loss or corruption of divine teachings. Fasting was prescribed for Jews and Christians as well as for Muslims.

REGULATIONS

Fasting in Ramadan is mandatory for every Muslim who is sane, adult, able, and resident. "Adult" is understood to be the age of puberty and discretion—about fourteen years old. Children under this age are encouraged to enter into the spirit of the month with partial abstinence on an easy level, so that when they reach the age of puberty they will be mentally and physically prepared to observe fasting.

"Able" means that the elderly and the chronically ill whose health is likely to be severely affected are excused. Nonetheless, such persons are required to provide an average full meal or its value to at least one poor person every day that he or she has missed fasting in Ramadan.

"Resident" means to be present at your permanent home or place of business and not to be on a journey of fifty to one hundred miles or more. And as noted above in the citation from the Qur'an, the ill and travelers can defer their fasting. The same applies to menstruating women, pregnant women, and mothers breastfeeding their children. They are to make up their fast at a later time, a day for a day.

The intention to fast should be made at night before going to sleep, but it can also be made upon awaking before dawn. A typical fasting day begins with getting up early, around 4:30 a.m., and eating before the fast begins at dawn, about 5:00 a.m. As dawn breaks, the first of five daily prayers is offered. Throughout the day, Muslims recall God's presence and seek God's mercy. The fast is broken as soon as the sun sets, with no delay; eating a few dates with water is traditional.

In observing these regulations, you should never lose sight of the fact that fasting is undertaken in obedience to and out of love for God. The fast of any day of Ramadan becomes void by intentionally eating, drinking, smoking, or engaging in sexual relations. If this is done deliberately without any lawful reason, it is a major sin that only renewed repentance can expiate. But if anyone, through forgetfulness, does something that would ordinarily break the fast, the observance is not nullified, and the fast stands valid, provided the person stops the moment realization occurs. Injection or intravenous treatment that is solely medical does not break the fast. In general, Muslims are permitted to break the ordained fast of Ramadan when there is danger to their health. In this case, they can make up the fast later at any other time of the year.

The lunar-year calendar is about ten or eleven days shorter than the Gregorian calendar. Thus, if Ramadan 2005 begins on October 5, Ramadan in 2006 begins on September 24. Consequently, in the course of thirty-six years, every Muslim would have fasted on both the short and the long days of the year, and during the hot months as well as the cooler months, whereas if the fast were based on the Gregorian calendar, some Muslims would fast long days every year and others shorter days, some always in hot weather and some always in mild or cold.

The much anticipated start of the month is based on a combination of physical sightings of the moon and astronomical calculations. The practice varies from place to place, some regions relying heavily on sighting reports and others totally on calculations. In the United States, most communities follow the decision of the Islamic Society of North America, which accepts confirmed sightings of the new moon anywhere in the United States as the start of the new month. The end of the month, marked by the celebration of Eid al-fitr, is similarly determined.

The reasons Muslims fast are multiple, and chief among them is the desire to sharpen awareness of God throughout the day, thereby pleasing God.

CULTIVATION OF ALLAH-CONSCIOUSNESS

The verse of the Qur'an that prescribes fasting among Muslims is: "O you who believe, fasting is prescribed for you as it is prescribed for those before you that you may guard against evil" (2:183). "Guard against evil" is a translation of the word *taqwaa*. It is derived from a word meaning "protective shield." The shield is alertness, vigilance in practicing Allah's commands, which protects the believer from all kinds of evil and corrupt and destructive forces. The Qur'an repeatedly promises that those who achieve *taqwaa* will gain the good of this life and the hereafter. When the Prophet's companion 'Umar was asked to explain the meaning of *taqwaa*, he illustrated it with a metaphor. A man trying to walk through a field of thickly planted thorn bushes holds his clothes close to his body and maneuvers carefully to avoid tearing his clothes and skin, always aware of the hazards. A person who achieves *taqwaa* is in a state of constant awareness of God. He thinks about how to please God by doing good and guarding against evil.[2] The rites and ordinances of Islam would be meaningless without the steadfast awareness of Allah.

Taqwaa is also sometimes translated as "piety" or "self-restraint." But these translations also relate to the meaning of the root word from which they come (protective shield). People are commanded to adopt fasting as a means to protect themselves against evil motives. Fasting safeguards you as an individual and the society as a whole. You are shielded by remaining alert to countermand the inclinations of your baser and self-serving instincts. Society is shielded from corrupting influences because when its individual members cultivate an awareness of the needs of others in the community, it contributes positively to the general welfare.

To this effect, the Prophet confirms in the Bukhari/Muslim hadith, "Fasting is like a shield (for protection from Satan's attack). Therefore when one observes the Fast, he should (use this shield and) abstain from quarreling. If anybody quarrels with him, he should simply say: 'Brother/Sister, I am fasting!' Allah does not have need of one's fasting; the fasting is for one's own good, that one may guard against evil."

But there is yet another level to the notion of fasting representing a protective shield. It brings the gift of Allah's Watch over the one who fasts.

> When the faster obeys Allah's commandments by rejecting the appeals of his desires that come to his mind during fasting, or when he trains himself to be patient every time he is tempted by delights and desires, out of feeling that Allah watches him and knows all the secrets of his heart; when he keeps on this for a full month (Ramadan), out of this continuous heed accompanying his activities, he certainly will attain the gift of Allah's Watch over him, as well as his own fear of the Lord. He will try to avoid the shameful situation of Allah's finding him where he is prohibited to be. Allah's Watch over him enables him to carry out all deeds of goodness, and keeps him away from evil. He then would not cheat, ill treat or do injustice to others; nor would he spread corruption among people.... The basic truth of fasting in Islam springs from Allah's Watch over the faster, as well as the latter's carrying out of his fast for the cause of none but Allah.[3]

DISCIPLINE AND TRAINING

In Islam, the talk around fasting is not peppered with words like "asceticism" or "mortification." There is, however, frequent reference to our animality and the need for discipline. Islam recognizes the great use to which animal urges can be put if they are properly trained and guided. Allah, the perfect Creator, has not created them in vain. But they have to be tamed.

> Now how do you tame an animal? Ask any circus manager. He will tell you that animals are tamed by denying them food and drink. Sex in the case of animals is seasonal. In the case of humans, it is perennial. That is why Islam has required that man should deny himself food, drink, and sex during the month of Ramadan. Study the life of all animals. Their only aim is to indulge in food, drink, and sex. Man is superior to all creation. In him lodges the divine spark in the soul, which can make him acquire divine virtues.... The animal urges within man, if brought under control and given the right direction, can lead to his moral and spiritual development.[4]

As for guidance after taming, the Qur'an is the guidebook: "I, Allah, am the Best Knower. This Book, there is no doubt in it, is a guide to those who guard against evil" (2:1, 2). The Qur'an not only teaches what errant human development can be but offers instruction in how to avoid it. Fasting enters here as a discipline enabling men and women to tame their animal urges and thus avoid exceeding the divine limits, beyond which lies evil. Ramadan is the month selected by Allah for this exercise in self-discipline. The goal is that the animality of people should become submissive to their spiritual side.

The cornerstone of *taqwaa* is developing a strong character by following the principles laid down by Allah in the Qur'an. A person who develops such a character, reflected in his or her actions, is a *muttaqi* in the eyes of Allah. Fasting is a means to becoming *muttaqi*. Ramadan provides the collective environment for the training and development of character. Muslims are required to emulate and display throughout the year qualities of compassion and fair play, perseverance and generosity. Since character-building is a hard, long, continuous process, Ramadan is repeated every year as a reminder and a reinforcer.[5]

Where the other pillars of Islam are concerned, the prayer *(salah)* lasts only a few minutes at a time; the charity tax *(zakah)* is paid only once a year. Although the time on the pilgrimage to Mecca *(hajj)* is long, it may come only once in a lifetime. But in the school of fasting, Muslims are trained to obey the injunctions of the law *(shariah)* for one full month every year, day and night.

A Muslim will have to get up before dawn for a little breakfast *(suhur),* stop all eating and drinking precisely at a given time, do certain activities and abstain from certain activities during the day, break the fast *(iftar)* in the evening at a certain time, and then proceed to the late evening prayers. A Muslim is like a soldier for a full month every year, living a disciplined life, and then he or she is sent to bring the fruits of this practice back into the normal routine of daily living for eleven months.

> The private nature of Fasting ensures that you have a strong faith in Allah as the One who knows everything. Only if your faith is true and strong, will you not dream of eating or drinking secretly: even in the hottest summer, when your throats dry up with thirst, you will not drink a drop of water; even when you feel faint with hunger, when life itself seems to be ebbing, you will not eat anything. To do all this, see what firm conviction you have that nothing whatsoever can ever be concealed from Allah! How strong must be His fear and love in your hearts. You will keep your Fast for about 360 hours for one full month only because of your profound belief in the reward and punishment of the Hereafter. Had you the slightest doubt that you have to meet your Maker, you would not complete such a Fast.[6]

The word *belief* in the Qur'an always means "belief with practice." The fast of Ramadan, like all the rites and ceremonies of Islam, is disciplinary.

> Our Lord has made us pilgrims to a shrine of most austere severity. Allah has made us pilgrims to an empty house. Islam, as compared with others, may be called a hard religion. There are no arm-chairs in it, no cushioned pews, no soothing music. There is nobody to do it for you; you must do it all yourself. Its rules are hard and fast, and there is no evading them. Its rites and ceremonies, few and simple, would not attract the kind of person, very common in our day, who seeks religion only to be put to rest, to give up thinking. Ours is a religion, not of slumber, but of energy.... And chief among its fortifying ordinances is the fast of Ramadan. An athlete, when he has to wrestle or to run a race, a soldier, when he has to go out and fight in hard conditions, fortifies himself beforehand by a course of training. And we, who have a greater match, a greater fight before us always—shall we not do our training as the Lord commands?[7]

The reference to "soldiers" and "army" is a recurring one. The institutions of Islam are designed for one purpose: to form righteous men and women and to bind them together in a brotherhood and sisterhood as compact and well disciplined as an army that may at any moment have to be mobilized. The kings of the world have their armies, the states of the world their police, but "we are the army of the living King who sleepeth not nor dieth, the Universal King to whom all return, whose judgement all the living have to face. It is well that there should be in the world a great community acknowledging a higher law than that of economic pressure, devoted to a service quite disinterested, supporting everywhere the cause of that justice of Allah, the king of all mankind, whose providence is over all alike, without distinction of wealth or poverty, race or creed."[8]

SOCIAL SOLIDARITY

Training of such a profound nature cannot be imparted to each individual separately. Just as all react together to the sound of the bugle in an army, everyone in the community of Allah learns to act in unison and to assist each other in their task of development. The month of Ramadan is thus a time when all Muslims fast together. It is a powerful expression of collective obedience and submission *(Ibadah)*. The moral and spiritual benefits accruing from the fasting by one person are increased a millionfold when a million fast together. Everyone makes a special effort to guard against evil and to avoid sin, and if they lapse, they know they can count on the help of many brothers and sisters who are fasting with them. It is easy to see where the expression "As flowers blossom in spring, so does *taqwaa* in Ramadan" came from. Feeding the poor, clothing the naked, helping those in distress, giving help where help is needed: The cumulative effect of such fervor could not but create an environment of social solidarity, a spirit of virtue and piety. Ramadan is the garden of virtue, and there are many who are watering the flowers.

Thus, as the time draws near, evening prayer attracts a larger number of worshipers than usual. People's eyes turn more frequently to the sky in an effort to sight the new moon that will inaugurate the month. When the new moon is sighted and the sighting confirmed, worshipers turn to one another with handshakes and knowing glances and the mosque is filled with the chants of *Allahu Akbar*—God is great!

Individual and personal spiritual development is not the purpose of fasting in Ramadan. The spirituality is communal. There is no going off to a mountaintop or forest retreat or desert monastery to develop a personal relationship with God. It is to happen in the streets and the homes and places of business. Islam's sense of itself as a "natural religion" contributes to this. The Prophet Muhammad is revered as an ordinary married man who, divested of the supernatural, ate food, walked in the streets, and brought religion back to its true sphere: the daily life of towns and cities. The light to which Allah leads believers is the light of every day. Allah's miracles are the miracles of day and night, life and death, the pageantry of the earth and the wonder of the stars at night. These are considered to be sufficient witness to the sovereignty of God, and there is no need to seek further.

This communal spirituality and solidarity are expressed through a social network in which resources are made available to help those who are left without protection or support in society; those who lose their means of livelihood or are incapacitated by work; those who cannot earn enough to meet their needs. This heightened sensitivity to the plight of unfortunates in the community is a direct result of the fasting. When a faster feels hungry, she is more mindful of those who are always hungry. The common hunger is an experience of poverty shared. Compassion is born from feeling one with the sufferer. On completion of Ramadan, the special charity (Sadaqat al-fitr) must be distributed before the breaking of the fast.

The social dimension of Ramadan is manifest at sunset each day. It is common practice to break the fast with dates (iftar), after the custom of the Prophet Muhammad. This is followed by the sunset prayer. Since everyone eats the evening meal at the same time, people often gather in each other's homes to share the meal.

BENEFITS AND REWARDS

Among the benefits commonly recognized in the observance of the fast of Ramadan is increased study and recitation of the Qur'an. Muslims are encouraged to try to read the whole book at least once during the month. Some will spend time each day listening to its recitation in a mosque.

There are also personal physiological health benefits. While Muslims do not fast because of medical benefits, the positive effects are nonetheless recognized. The prescribed fast is different from various diet plans because it has features of both a fast and a diet. Shahid Athar, MD, ascribes its unique medical benefits to several factors.[9] First, Ramadan does not cause malnutrition or inadequate calorie intake since there is no restriction on the type or amount of food intake before beginning the fast at sunrise or ending it at sunset.

Second, fasting in Ramadan is voluntarily undertaken, as opposed to being a prescribed imposition from a physician. In the hypothalamus part of the brain, there is a center called the lipostat that controls body mass. When severe and rapid weight loss is achieved by a starvation diet, the lipostat does not recognize this as normal and therefore reprograms itself to cause rapid weight gain once the person goes off the starvation diet. So the only effective way of losing weight is slow, self-controlled, and gradual weight loss, which can be achieved by modifying attitudes about food and eating patterns, especially by eliminating excess food. Ramadan is a month of self-regulation and self-training, thereby potentially effecting a stable change in lipostat reading.

Third, those who fast are not subjected to a diet of selective food, for example, only protein or only carbohydrates. Breakfast is taken before dawn, and at sunset the fast is broken with something sweet like dates, fruit, and juices to offset any hypoglycemia, followed by a regular dinner later on.

Fourth, after dinner Muslims go to their mosque to offer the *Isha* prayer, the fourth of the five daily prayers. The day ends with a special voluntary prayer, the *Taraweeh,* offered by the congregation reciting the Qur'an. These prayers involve physical movement, which helps metabolize the food. The special night prayer of Ramadan, as well as the five daily prescribed prayers, use all the muscles and joints and are a mild form of exercise.

Fifth, the month moderates habits. Those who chain smoke, nibble food constantly, or drink several cups of coffee daily experience life without these habits and may leave them behind.

And finally, many attest to a psychological effect of increased peace and tranquility. Dr. Shahid reports that he usually checks his own blood glucose, cholesterol, and triglyceride levels when Ramadan begins and when it ends, and there is marked improvement. As mentioned earlier, the sick and those with chronic health conditions that would be exacerbated by fasting are exempt.

More substantial than these secondary benefits, however, is the spiritual reward. It is reported that the Prophet said:

> He who fasts during Ramadan with faith and seeks his reward from Allah will have his past sins forgiven; he who prays during the night in Ramadan with faith and seeks his reward from Allah will have his past sins forgiven; and he who passes Lailat al-Qadr (the Night of Power) in prayer with faith and seeks his reward from Allah will have his past sins forgiven. (Bukhari/Muslim hadith)[10]

In addition to the promise that you will be forgiven, there is another incentive in the month's final stage. The last ten days of Ramadan are a time of particular intensity and focus on God and the performance of good deeds. The night on which the first verses of the Qur'an were revealed to the Prophet, known as the Night of Power (Lailat al-Qadr), is generally taken to be the twenty-seventh night of the month. As the Qur'an states that this night is better than a thousand months, many Muslims spend the entire night in prayer.

The greatest reward, however, is to know that you have given pleasure to Allah through all your efforts.

Allah is our Creator, the Lawgiver who is going to revive us after death and to demand accounts of our actions in the present world. Whoever will have obeyed Him, shall obtain His pleasure, even if we have not understood the underlying secrets of His commandments. The fasting enjoined by a religion, by a revealed law must entail divine pleasure if we accomplish it. And what spiritual and worldly benefit can be greater than the eternal pleasure of our Lord? Material motives should not be allowed to mar the purity of the intention. Let our fast be wholly and solely for the pleasure and in compliance with the demands of Allah.[11]

In summary, there is a veritable litany of overall spiritual benefits that can be ascribed to fasting in Islam:

- Teaches the principle of sincere love because we fast out of a deep love for God
- Equips us with an optimistic sense of hope because we are hoping to please God and seeking God's grace
- Imbues us with effective devotion and a feeling of closeness to God
- Cultivates a sound conscience because the integrity of our fast is not something others can verify but is between God and ourselves
- Inculcates the virtue of patience because we feel the pains of deprivation but endure them patiently throughout the day
- Strengthens our willpower and healthy self-control
- Provides us with an experience of moderation and temperance
- Helps us realize we are all equal before God, as well as before the law
- Surrounds us with the inspiration and support of a community of faith[12]

After the thirty days of fasting, the end of the month is observed with a day of celebration called Eid al-fitr. On this day, Muslims from around the village, town, or city gather in one place to offer a prayer of thanks. It is traditional to wear new clothes, visit friends and relatives, exchange gifts, and eat delicious dishes specially prepared for the occasion. Muslims use various phrases to congratulate one another at the Eid al-fitr festival. Most common are "May you be well throughout the year" *(Kullu am wa antum bi-khair)* or "A Blessed Eid!" *(Eid mubarak)*.

Outside Ramadan, there are other times recommended for voluntary fasting following the traditions of the Prophet. Among them are Mondays and Thursdays of every week, a few days in each of the two months heralding the coming of Ramadan, and on the sixth day following the festival of Eid al-fitr. The only days of the year when fasting is prohibited are Fridays and the feasts of Eid al-fitr and Eid al-'adha. While it is understood that the only obligatory fast is that of Ramadan, regular fasting throughout the year is encouraged to help maintain the Allah-consciousness achieved in Ramadan.

KEEPING THE SPIRIT OF THE PRACTICE ALIVE

This chapter began by stating that Islam aims to transform the whole of human life into a life of worship. The real purpose of the ritual acts of prayer five times daily, the contribution to charity, the fasting, and the pilgrimage to Mecca is to help us come to that life where the awareness of Allah pervades our consciousness. S. A. Mawdudi stresses it in plain terms:

> Never think that you can acquit yourselves of what you owe to Allah only if you bow and prostrate yourselves five times a day, suffer hunger and thirst from dawn to sunset for thirty days in Ramadan and, if wealthy, give alms and perform the Pilgrimage once in your lifetime. Doing all

this does not release you from the bondage to Him, nor make you free to do whatever you like. Rather, one of the underlying purposes of enjoining these rituals upon you is to develop you so that you can transform your whole lives into *Ibadah* (obedient submission) of Allah.[13]

Every work has two essential components. The first is its purpose and spirit; the second is the particular form that is chosen to achieve that purpose. Every religion shares in the struggle to keep the purpose clearly focused and to stave off rote practice in the form. Citing the words of the Prophet Muhammad, "Many are the people who fast, but who gain nothing from their fast except hunger and thirst; and many are those who stand praying all night but who gain nothing except sleeplessness," Mawdudi worries that some Muslims

have practically changed the meaning of *Ibadah.* Many of us believe that mere abstention from food and drink from morning to evening amounts to *Ibadah,* that once you have done all these things you have worshiped Allah. A greater majority of the Muslims is unmindful of the real spirit of *Ibadah* which should permeate all our actions. That is why the acts of *Ibadah* do not produce their full benefit. For everything in Islam depends on intention and understanding....

Perhaps we can now understand why our *Ibadah* has become ineffectual and empty. The greatest mistake of all is to take the acts of Prayer and Fasting and their outward shape as the real *Ibadah.* Otherwise, how can we explain that a person who is fasting, and is thus engaged in the *Ibadah* of Allah from morning till evening, in the midst of that *Ibadah,* tells a lie or slanders someone? Why does he quarrel on the slightest pretext and abuse those he is quarreling with?...

How, too, can we claim to have worshiped Allah for many long hours throughout Ramadan when the impact of this whole exercise in spiritual and moral upliftment vanishes on the first day of the next month? During the Eid [Eid al-fitr festival] days we do all that pagans do in their festivals, so much so that in some places we even turn to adultery, drinking, and gambling. And I have seen some degenerates who Fast during the day and drink alcohol and commit adultery at night. Most Muslims ... have not fallen so low. But how many of us still retain any trace of piety and virtue by the second day of Eid?[14]

Dr. Abu Ameenah Bilal Philips paints an even more dramatic picture of the dangers of observing the form and losing sight of the purpose:

Many Muslims fast in a way that technically qualifies as fasting, but in reality achieves none of the goals of fasting. They gorge themselves at sunset on delicacies that no one bothers to prepare the rest of the year. Instead of praying extra prayers they play cards or engage in less wholesome diversions and snack and drink through the night before gorging themselves once again just before dawn. They then crawl into their beds like a python that has just swallowed a whole sheep. They may or may not pray the dawn prayer. They may wake up at noon. Some of them only wake shortly before sunset, just in time to prepare themselves for another night of festivities.[15]

Jews will hear in these words echoes of Isaiah 58:5 in which God angrily asks, "Is this the fast I want?" Catholics will recognize here the reasons post–Vatican II bishops transmuted the obligation of the Friday practice into a voluntary one, encouraging church members to rediscover the *spirit* of the weekly fast day. And Eastern Orthodox Christians, for whom the form still claims half the days on their church calendar, will find an invitation to look into their own hearts to see how clearly the original meaning of the fast days still burns. The form that has been prescribed for the cultivation of Allah-consciousness finds various applications among the children of Abraham, but one thing holds true for them all: Fasting only proves valuable as a spiritual practice when consciousness of its purpose permeates the heart and mind and finds consistent expression in thoughts, words, and deeds.

A LIVING VOICE FROM THE TRADITION

Ibrahim Negm is the imam of the Islamic Center of the South Shore in Long Island, New York. He was appointed as the religious leader there in 1996. While we were together for the annual Catholic-Muslim Mid-Atlantic Dialogue, I took the opportunity to interview him on fasting in Islam.

> *One of the primary functions of the mosque is the observance of the fast in the ninth month of the Islamic calendar, Ramadan. What is your experience of Ramadan?*
>
> It's quite a vibrant experience for myself and for my community, because what usually happens in the month of Ramadan is that people change their routine. As we know, Muslims are living in America, and the schedule is not accommodating for Muslims because they have to go on with their regular work lives. There's no special holiday for them, so they have to change their routine a little bit to allow more concentration on worship and spiritual pursuits. And this is quite an experience for the whole

family, as a matter of fact. Usually what the people do is that they plan ahead for the coming of the fast. They try to free their minds from the worldly concerns and try to focus on the guest that's coming—that's the month of Ramadan, which is so special for Muslims in so many ways.

First and foremost, of course, is the chance of retreat—retreat toward God, thinking more about their inner selves, thinking more about the needy and the poor, thinking more about the suffering of the hungry and the less fortunate people. And also it's a chance for them to renew their commitment to the Qur'an, which is the scripture of God because it is during this month—more specifically on the twenty-seventh night—that the beginning of the Qur'an was revealed. The first portion of the Qur'an was revealed in the month of Ramadan, so the month of Ramadan is an opportunity to witness to this divine intervention in the world. This is a chance to also look into the Qur'an and honor it in so many ways. You will find a lot of Muslims, particularly the imams or the religious leaders, paying more attention to the Qur'an during this month. They honor it in a special prayer called *Taraweeh*.

Taraweeh prayer, which is offered usually after *Isha* prayer, is the night prayer, or the fifth prayer of the day. They usually recite one whole part of the Qur'an. While the Qur'an is divided into thirteen parts, they read one part each night. Usually the custom is that by the end of the month of Ramadan, they complete reading the Qur'an. In many mosques, like my own, the imam usually does a little explanation, sort of a synopsis, a reflection that people listen to for about half an hour. After that, usually people have a get-together for *iftar*, or breaking of the fast. You'll find this custom in every mosque.

Wherever you are, if you are nearby a mosque, then it usually is your obligation to just stop by and have a little something to break your fast.

After that, you do the *Maghrib* prayer, which is a prayer that is done at the sunset time. Other than that there is also a special charity, which each fasting person usually gives to the poor and the needy, reinforcing, of course, the social solidarity among Muslims. Ramadan offers a chance to get to know the religion of Islam, so you'll find a lot of Muslims, especially during this month, going to bookstores and trying to get some books that will help them in their spiritual quest. You'll find this is the high season for the bookstore owners because it's usually during this month that they sell most of the books and videotapes about Islam and also some software programs, especially those for the kids. So it's a chance for all Muslims to learn more about their religion.

You will especially find Muslims making an extra effort during the last ten days of Ramadan. This is primarily because they are promised such great rewards during one special night. It's called the Night of Power or Lailat al-Qadr—the night in which the beginning of the Qur'an was revealed. So there is special significance to this night, and Muslims are promised great rewards if they observe that night with prayer and fasting and reading more from the Qur'an.

After the month of Ramadan, we have a major celebration that's called Eid, which is a day of joy and happiness for all the Muslim community. It's also a day of thanksgiving to God because he has empowered us to observe the fast and to give charity for the Muslims. So it's marked by a morning prayer, which is called Eid prayer, and is followed by a sermon that is usually given by the imam on that day. The theme is one of reinforcing the spirit of gratitude and thanks, thanking God for his immense blessings.

What is the spirit among the people on that day of breaking the fast after having lived such an intense experience together for a full month?

The spirit is one of utmost joy and also of an immense level of solidarity and cohesion because for a whole month they had a chance to go to the mosques. Usually the mosques during the month of Ramadan are filled up, and you will not find a spot. So people generally come a lot earlier for the prayer than what usually takes place on the days other than the month of Ramadan, because they come together and they have a chance to socialize at the mosques, to get to know each other. And on the day of breaking the fast, which is Eid al-fitr day, you will find this spirit of togetherness and solidarity and cohesion among the people. They develop new acquaintances every Ramadan. It is also a time of immense joy, especially for the kids, because they cannot relate to most of the major holidays in the country, especially at Christmas or Hanukkah, so this is *their* Muslim function, and they are extra happy and joyous.

Do Muslims fast at any other time of the year? On any other days outside Ramadan?

Yes, there are two categories of fasting—the obligatory fasting and the voluntary fasting. Obligatory fasting is during the whole month of Ramadan. There is voluntary fasting outside Ramadan. The Prophet himself used to observe Mondays and Thursdays for fasting. So, you'll find also Muslims following that tradition. There are also special days during the year other than the month of Ramadan for which Prophet Muhammad gave a special, strong advice for the Muslims to keep the fast on these certain days, so you'll find that custom also being practiced by a lot of Muslims.

And what would the fast day look like on one of those voluntary days? Would it still be from sunrise to sunset? Or would they modify that in some way?

No. It's the same for everybody—the same regulations. If you want to fast, it's the same conditions. You ought to stay away from food, drink, and sexual intercourse from dawn to sunset. So, it doesn't matter. The format does not change.

How does the rhythm of people's lives change when they are fasting during Ramadan? Is it a month in which they go to bed later, get up earlier or later in the morning? Eat larger or smaller breakfasts and suppers?

It usually depends on where the Muslims happen to be. For those in the North American context, it's a regular workday in a non-Muslim culture, so there is no special accommodation for the schedule of fast. So Muslims usually have a hard time during this month because, on the one hand, they have to observe the fast and focus themselves spiritually; but at the same time, their work schedule is not accommodating, so they end up having less sleep and, of course, more spiritual quests. I advise my congregation—because they usually spend one or two hours commuting back and forth in their cars or on the train—to take that chance to read more from the Qur'an, to read more prayers, and to try to utilize the precious time of Ramadan because Muslims are promised immense rewards if they do good deeds during this month. So, usually, yes, they have difficulty coping with the environment, but they end up having more rewards because they work on themselves and they try to do good deeds, so this brings inner joy for them.

What would some of these rewards be, for example?

The Prophet Muhammad said that if you do one single good deed in the month of Ramadan, usually it is multiplied into seventy good deeds. Also a lot of Muslims prefer to make a minor pilgrimage to Mecca during the month of Ramadan because the Prophet himself said that if you do it, it would be upgraded to a full-fledged *hajj* or pilgrimage. Similarly, if you give charity, you will get more rewards. This is a special time for Muslims to be charitable.

When you say rewards, are you thinking of concrete rewards, like riches or good health, or are you thinking more just in terms of God's grace?

It's actually both. The meaning of reward means you might get a concrete material reward in this world and you would also get God's grace and forgiveness in the hereafter. So it works both ways.

If you had to summarize the "why" of fasting for a Muslim, what would you say? What is the essential motivation?

The primary motivation is to please God. There are other considerations than that, but they come secondary to this primary motivation, which is to please God. Basically, as Muslims, if we find something written in the Qur'an, we are supposed to listen and obey. So that's the primary motivation: to please God. The other secondary motivations are there—to work on yourself, to fight your own whims and desires, to solidify the community, to try to feel the pains of the hungry people—but all of these are secondary motivations. The primary motivation of why Muslims fast is to please God.

CHAPTER FIVE

HINDUISM: PURITY, RESPECT, PENANCE

Hinduism is one of the oldest religions in the world, but it has no identifiable founder because it is a religion that evolved and developed through the centuries from the spiritual, religious, and social practices of the people of the Indian subcontinent. Although it has sacred writings, there is no specific book or particular spiritual path to follow. Each person is allowed to find and choose the path, the devotions, and the practices that best suit him or her given his or her current status in life, abilities, needs, and interests. A person may thus be guided by a guru, a book, a tradition of practice, or personal conscience. Fasting in the context of the lives of Hindus reflects all these realities.

European colonists invented the word *Hinduism* to refer to the spiritual and social practices of the people of India. Hindus themselves use Sanatana Dharma or "the eternal, universal tradition of righteousness and duty" to describe their practices.

Hindus consider Brahman (sometimes referred to as Isvara) the ultimate reality. There are hundreds of divine manifestations of the supreme in Hinduism. These manifestations, *devas* and *devis,* or gods and goddesses, personify aspects of Brahman. The three main gods representing the Hindu trinity are Brahma, the creator; Vishnu, the force for preservation; and Shiva, the destructive force. All reality is an expression or manifestation of Brahman, the one that is all.

The primary Hindu sacred writings are the Vedas, which means "knowledge" in Sanskrit, the ancient language of the Hindus. They are the oldest texts known, and they are understood to contain universal truth. There are four Vedic books, the Rigveda being the most important among them. Other collections of sacred writings are the Upanishads, the Puranas, and two of the world's greatest epic spiritual works: the Ramayana and the Mahabharata (the Bhagavad Gita is but a part of the latter).

FASTING IN HINDUISM

The Sanskrit word for fasting is *upavasa. Upa* means "near" and *vasa* means "to stay." Implicit in the word is that fasting means "to stay near (the Lord)," to keep the Lord close in your heart and mind. The very word for fasting thus has an inbuilt orientation to the Divine.

Most devout Hindus fast regularly or on special occasions such as festivals honoring particular gods and goddesses. On religious holidays, they do not eat at all, eat once, or limit themselves to fruit or a special diet of simple food. In other words, the approach to fasting reflects the broad range of possibilities that characterizes Hinduism itself. The practice of fasting ranges from complete abstinence from any food or drink to abstinence from solid food with an occasional drink of water, milk, or juice, to abstinence from certain foods, such as salt. Each person finds a way of working with practices of his or her choosing.

There are, however, some traditional days for fasting, such as on Purnima (full moon) and Ekadasi, the eleventh day after the full moon and the new moon (once a fortnight). On these special days, devotees fast and make an extra effort to render devotional service. Fasting on Ekadasi, if observed strictly, involves taking no food or water from the previous day's sunset until forty-eight minutes after the following day's sunrise. Whereas the earth's rotation around the sun takes twenty-four hours, by the Indian lunar calendar it takes sixty *nazhikas,* or units of time; the forty-eight minutes is an extra *nazhika* just to make sure that the lunar rotation is complete and the new day has begun. The Ekadasi days are a time to step back from your normal routine and take stock of your spiritual life. Common practices are fasting from grains and legumes, chanting, reading, avoiding strenuous physical labor and long-distance travel, as well as avoiding activities relating to the body, such as laundry, shaving, and food shopping.

In general, Hindus engage in fasting for one or more of three reasons: physical and mental purity, as a sign of respect for a god or goddess, and to do penance.

PURITY

In Hindu philosophy everything is marked by three qualities or *gunas: sattva* (purity), *rajas* (passion), and *tamas* (inertia). When something is pure and calm, the *sattva guna* is dominant; when restless, agitated, or angry, it is the *rajas guna* that is manifesting; and when sleepy, lazy, or lethargic, it is the *tamas guna* that has come to the fore. This also applies to types of food and their effect on us.

In the Bhagavad Gita, Lord Krishna declares that food is of three types: *Sattvic* food—nutritious, fresh, juicy—increases purity, longevity, strength, health, and happiness; *rajasic* food— hot, salty, spicy, sour, or bitter—sows unhappiness, sorrow, and disease; and *tamasic* food—leftovers, food that is stored, stale, smelly—is hard to digest and leads to inertia.

In other words, certain types of food contribute to our well-being, while others leave us feeling dis-eased. As we spend a lot of time shopping for food, preparing it, eating it, and digesting it, there may be certain days when we simply decide to save time and conserve energy by eating either simple, light food or totally abstaining from eating altogether to clear away the mental clutter and become more alert. The mind, otherwise preoccupied with food, can now "stay near the Lord." The more we indulge the senses, the more they make clamorous demands. Exerting a certain control over the sensual appetites frees the mind to pass more easily to contemplation. Fasting helps us cultivate control over the senses and keeps the mind peaceful. When the stomach is full, the digestive system draws the blood circulation toward the digestive organs, decreasing blood circulation to the head and inducing sleep. Fasting keeps the stomach free and the body light and is conducive to meditation.

Thus it is that those who practice yoga, for example, will be careful to eat the kinds of food that will cultivate purity, clarity, balance, and peace, because these are the foundations for deep concentration in meditation as well as for health in general. So the practice of fasting is one of many yogic techniques for cultivating *sattva*. Fasting is understood to create attunement with the Absolute by establishing a harmonious relationship between the body and the soul.

The ancient epic Mahabharata says:

> It was by fasts that the deities have succeeded in becoming denizens of heaven. It is by fasts that the Rishis have attained to high success. Chyavana and Jamadagni and Vasishtha and Gautama and Brigu—all these great Rishis endued with the virtue of forgiveness, have attained to heaven through observance of fasts. In former days Angirasa declared so unto the great Rishis. The man who teaches another the merit of fasts has never to suffer any kind of misery. The man who daily reads these ordi-

nances [about fasts], or hears them read, becomes freed
from sins of every kind.[1]

On a physiological level, every system needs a break, a
housecleaning day, to function well. The cleansing properties of
a fasting day are good for the digestive system and the entire
body. In its own way, fasting contributes to physical purity
through the elimination of accumulated waste in the body. The
ancient Indian medical system of Ayurveda sees the basic cause
of many diseases as the accumulation of toxic materials in the
digestive system. Regular cleansing of toxic materials keeps us
healthy. In moderate fasting, the organs of the body are cleansed
and renewed.

You should not overdo fasting. It is supposed to make you
feel buoyant, not fatigued. You should only practice as much
fasting as your capacity allows. If you cannot do service because
of fasting, you are better off eating.[2]

RESPECT

Devout Hindus observe fasting on special occasions as a mark of
respect to their personal deities. Consistent with the meaning of
fasting *(upavasa)* as staying near to the Lord, individuals choose
particular days to be near their favorite god or goddess. On that
day, control of all the senses is exercised, not just that of taste. It
is like a retreat day or day of recollection, and devotees may
withdraw from regular activities, go to the temple, or find a
secluded place for their devotions. It cannot be adequately cate-
gorized simply as a "fast day," but it will generally include some
form of fasting in the devotee's observance of vows made to the
designated deity. On a particular religious holiday or festival
day, for example, a person may choose to generate peaceful
energy by meditating or chanting mantras. Fasting can be an
integral part of the devotee's approach to the day and manner of
living it.

One of the best examples of how fasting is part of a larger picture are the votive fasting rites called *vrats*. They are practiced throughout India and their observance spans social classes and caste and sectarian affiliations. Once again, there is a great variety in the kinds of *vrats* performed as well as numerous variations in the actual practice of any particular kind of *vrat*. In general they are performed by married women as a votive prayer for the benefit of their husband and children.

The *vrats* most commonly performed are on Monday to Shiva, on Tuesday to Ganapati, on Wednesday to Krishna, on Thursday to Dattaguru, on Friday to Lakshmi, on Saturday to Hanuman, and on Sunday to Surya. There are also the Sri Satyanarayan *vrat* and the Karva Chauth *vrat*. On the occasion of Karva Chauth, for example, a fasting *vrat* is observed. In a typical rite, a small container is filled with either milk or water. Five pieces of different metals (gold, silver, copper, brass, and iron) are placed in the container and presented to Brahman (no prayer is complete unless it is accompanied by an offering). While presenting the container, the wife prays for her husband and their marriage and family. Part of her offering that day will be her fast.

More broadly, fasting at festivals (practically all festivals in India are marked by a religious character) is common. Hindus all over India observe fasts on festivals such as Shivratri and Karva Chauth. Navaratri is a festival when people fast for nine days.

The hunger experienced on these occasions always renders the heart more compassionate toward the destitute who often go without food. Hindus believe that serving food to the poor and the needy brings good karma. Food is often distributed to people at the end of many religious ceremonies, and many Hindu temples distribute food freely every day to visiting devotees.

PENANCE

When the words *fasting* and *India* are put together, the first person who comes to mind is Mahatma Gandhi. Most people would likely characterize his fasts, however, as actions of social protest. While in some instances that was true, what most people are not aware of is the penitential nature of many of Gandhi's fasts. According to the Gandhi Institute's compilation and publication of correspondence and records around the Mahatma's declared fasts, fully half of them were embraced by him in a personal spirit of atonement.[3] Even the public fasts associated with the religious movement of *satyagraha,* in which he sought to secure reforms or redress of grievances by self-suffering, were perceived by him as a process of purification and penance. I present here a sampling of some of his correspondence as the best example possible of fasting as penance in the Hindu tradition.

On February 2, 1921, Gandhi wrote to a friend:

> I have heard that you have gone on hunger strike at not finding sufficient response from your neighbor to the call of non-co-operation. Whilst your action shows the purity of your heart and the spirit of sacrifice, in my opinion, it is hasty and possibly thoughtless. Fasting for the purpose of showing one's displeasure or disappointment can hardly be justified. Its basis must be penance or purification.

On November 18, 1921, the Prince of Wales arrived in Bombay, and demonstrations against his visit, including a bonfire of foreign-made cloth, resulted in riots on a large scale. The following day, a dejected Gandhi, who had hoped for a peaceful protest atmosphere, issued a message in leaflet form, which said, in part:

> Nor can I shirk my own personal responsibility. I am more instrumental than any other in bringing into being the spirit of revolt. I find myself not fully capable of controlling and disciplining that spirit. I must do penance for it. For me the struggle is essentially religious. I believe in

fasting and prayer, and I propose henceforth to observe every Monday a twenty-four hour's fast till *swaraj* is attained.

On September 18, 1924, his doctor, alarmed that Gandhi was becoming weaker and concerned for his health, pleaded with Gandhi to tell him why he was engaging in this fast. And Gandhi replied:

> I launched non-co-operation. Today I find that people are non-co-operating against one another, without any regard for nonviolence. What is the reason? Only this, that I myself am not completely nonviolent. If I were practicing nonviolence to perfection, I should not have the violence I see around me today. My fast is therefore a penance. I blame no one. I blame only myself. I have lost the power where-with to appeal to people. Defeated and helpless I must submit petition in His Court. Only He [God] will listen, no one else....
>
> M. D.: But, Bapu, should the penance take only this shape, and no other? Is fasting prescribed by our religion?
>
> Gandhi: Certainly, what did the rishis [sages] of old do? It is unthinkable that they ate anything during their penance—in some cases, gone through in caves and for hundreds of years. Parvati who did penance to win Siva would not touch even the leaves of trees, much less fruit or food [story from Hindu mythology]. Hinduism is full of penance and prayer.

On September 21, 1924, Gandhi wrote:

> My helplessness is a very patent fact before me. I may not ignore it. I must ever confess it. There is a beautiful Tamil proverb that says: "God is the sole help of the help-

less." The truth of this never came upon me with much force as it has come today. Handling large masses of men, dealing with them, speaking and acting for them is no joking matter for a man whose capacity God has so circumscribed. One has, therefore, to be ever on the watch. The reader may rest assured that I took the final step after I had realized to the full my utter helplessness. And I cried out to God. That cry must not be from the lip. It has to be from the deepest recesses of one's heart. And, therefore, such a cry is only possible when one is in anguish. Mine has expressed itself in a fast, which is by no means adequate, for the issues involved. My heart continually says: Rock of Ages cleft for me / Let me hide myself in Thee.

And as a final example of the spirit of penance and purification that characterized his fasts, this response to the letter of a friend on September 30, 1924:

Thank you for your letter. I am daily praying to God to guide me. It was after prayer that I began the fast. I have taken it up not to die but to live a better and purer man for service; but if God wills otherwise who can help? I quite agree with you that unity cannot be achieved by human effort in one day, but faith and prayer can work miracles.

A LIVING VOICE FROM THE TRADITION

Swami Vasishta, who shares his thoughts on Hindu fasting here, is a priest at the Sivananda yoga ashram in Woodbourne, New York.

Fasting in Hinduism is all personal. People—not all—will normally fast twice in a month. In India we follow the path of the moon in our calendar. Hindus will fast on Ekadasi days—after the eleventh day of all new and full moons. In the early scriptures, called Shruthi (Upanishads), we do not have any reference about fasting. It all came later in the era of Puranas. There fasting is mentioned as *tapas* or discipline—the control of all the sense organs. Generally people observe this kind of discipline, including fasting, on particular days dedicated for a special occasion for his or her god or goddess. For example, Sivarathri is very auspicious for the Siva devotees, Janmashtami is auspicious for Krishna devotees, Ramnavami for the devotees of Ram, and so on. On this day, they observe fasting and do good deeds, which include giving food for brahmins and almsgiving for the poor.

Fasting is not a strict discipline in Hinduism with rules that everyone must follow. As I mentioned, it is all personal. There is nothing compulsory to any of this fasting. For example, in southern India, the main ingredient of the food is rice. People eat rice generally at each meal, but on the day of *upavasa,* they will not eat rice, though they might eat all other things. Other people will observe their fast by eating just one meal during the day. Still others may eat only fruits and milk. So we cannot say what fasting really is for people. In Hinduism, fasting is not an isolated activity. It is usually done in the context of a vow. And people make different kinds of vows in their efforts to draw close to a particular god.

In India we practice Ayurvedic medicine. When someone is ill, the appropriate food will be determined by the doctor according to the illness; but generally the sick person eats something every day. I have not heard of any Ayurvedic physicians advising long fasts.

The main idea of fasting or *upavasa* came from the Mahabhagavatgha Purana. There we see a reference that those who completely observed fasting on Ekadasi day were saved by the god Mahavishnu. So the old people or very strict devotees see this incident in the Purana and try to observe fasting. It will be mainly the devotees of Vishnu who observe this Ekadasi. Again, it is a very personal practice.

In Hindusm, the fasting we do all has a very spiritual purpose. In the West it seems oftentimes purely physical. People might only think of fasting, for example, when they have problems of digestion or when they want to lose weight. But it is not something that is done on special religious days. There seems to be no spiritual motivation in fasting.

In Hinduism, in the path of spirituality all observances—vows, chanting, meditation, silence, fasting, and the like—are personal and undertaken for individual reasons: some for going to heaven, some for just pleasing the *devas* or *devis,* some for the blessings, and some for doing penance. But they all have the same goal—*upavasam,* to stay near to the Lord.

CHAPTER SIX

BUDDHISM: PURITY OF BODY, CLARITY OF MIND, MODERATION

Buddhism holds a distinctive place among the religions of the world because its founder, Shakyamuni Buddha, did not profess to be either an incarnation of God or sent by God. In fact, he had no interest in religious speculation about God and repudiated the very notion of an independent creator of the world. He simply claimed to be awakened or enlightened and sought to show others the path to liberation. He taught only what he had experienced by direct knowledge, and he encouraged others to develop such knowledge themselves. He claimed that he had discerned the *dharma*—the ground of the path of salvation, the Truth that is the basis of all truth and the guide for living—which opened up the secret of life and liberation.

When you think of religion, you probably presume that theistic belief or faith in God is part of the picture. Although this is not the case with Buddhism, it is nevertheless considered a religion in the sense that it offers a philosophical psychology or worldview by which to interpret experiences, and a coherent system of practice with which followers can order their lives and come to liberation—which is the core meaning of the word *salvation* as used by other religions. When a philosophy becomes a guiding principle for your life, when it gives you a process for transformation, it becomes a religion. Confucianism, Taoism, and Buddhism all qualify here, even though they hold no theistic belief.

Before becoming enlightened, the Buddha was known as Siddhartha Gautama. A minimal familiarity with his personal story is necessary to understand how fasting is perceived within Buddhism. Siddartha Gautama (circa 566–486 BCE) was the son of a king who ruled the lands at the foot of the Himalayas, along what is today the border between India and Nepal. Leaving home at age twenty-nine, Siddhartha gave up his princely life and became a wandering ascetic, seeking the answer to the question of why people get sick, grow old, and die. In short, he sought a satisfactory answer to why people suffer.

Disillusioned with the life of the palace, he went to the forest, gave his horse and jewelry away, and cut off his hair as a sign of renouncing the world. The forest was the place for seeking wisdom about the proper path for humans in the world. He met there a group of ascetics doing penance in the hope of a happy rebirth in heaven. After spending some time with them, he became disillusioned with the forest-dwelling ascetics as well. All worlds—including heaven—in Indian belief are subject to change, so what the ascetics were seeking (a happy rebirth in heaven) was only a temporary solution. Siddhartha sought not simply a better place in the cycle of change, but a lasting liberation.

So he set off to study with different masters. After learning what they had to teach him, he still did not believe that he had found the way to liberation. When he encountered five mendicants along the way, he was inspired once again to take up the ascetic life and practiced difficult austerities and fasting. For six years he dedicated himself to this path, taking only the barest

minimum of food and drink. Physically weakened and emaci-
ated, he decided in the end that this was not the way to liberation. He remembered an earlier experience in his life when he
had sat under a rose apple tree and attained firmness of mind
through meditation, and he reflected that this was the true way
and he must return to it. To follow this path, he realized, would
require physical and mental strength; thus he must eat and drink
for nourishment. He abandoned rigorous asceticism and went
down to the river to wash off the dirt that Indian ascetics cover
themselves with, thereby symbolically rejecting the extremes
that characterized this path. When he came out of the river, he
drank some milk that a young woman offered him, which
restored his physical health and strength and enabled him to
now attain to the highest knowledge.

Soon thereafter he sat under the Bodhi tree in meditation
and achieved victory over inner temptation, passions, and mental afflictions to finally break through to real wisdom, the ability
to see clearly the real nature of the world in the cycle of causa-
tion. In his night of enlightenment, the Buddha came to understand the Four Noble Truths and the Eightfold Path, which
would form the core of his teaching.[1]

BUDDHIST FASTING PRACTICE TODAY

Given the experience and conclusions of the Buddha about the
extremes of asceticism, one would expect to find the value of
moderation firmly ensconced in Buddhist spiritual practice, and
such is the case. There is an appreciation for the contribution that
fasting can make as a method of purification and as a method for
practicing self-control, but care is taken to avoid extremes.

All the main branches of Buddhism practice some periods
of fasting, usually on full moon days and other holidays.
Theravada and Tendai Buddhist monks fast as a means of free-
ing the mind. Some Tibetan monks fast to generate inner heat.
Fasting usually means abstaining from solid food, with some

liquids permitted, although this can vary depending on the Buddhist tradition. The Buddha advised monks not to take solid food after noon, which remains in practice today. Laypeople who observe the eight precepts also abstain on full moon days from taking any solid food after noon.

A LIVING VOICE FROM THE TRADITION

I called on one of my colleagues in the North American Monastic Interreligious Dialogue, Reverend Heng Sure, PhD, for a firsthand account of Buddhist fasting practice today. Reverend Heng Sure is the director of the Berkeley Buddhist Monastery, president of the Dharma Realm Buddhist Association, and Senior Monastic Bhikshu of the late Chan master Hsuan Hua. He has been a Buddhist monk in the Chinese Mahayana tradition for twenty-nine years and received all his training in the United States at Gold Mountain Monastery in San Francisco and at the City of Ten Thousand Buddhas in Talmage, California. He teaches Buddhist-Christian dialogue at the Graduate Theological Union in Berkeley.

Does fasting hold a very significant place in Buddhist spiritual practice?

First of all, before I even begin, I want to emphasize that my comments do not represent *the* Buddhist approach to fasting; certainly within the large, global Buddhist family with all its diversity, there are many, many different attitudes and practices. My comments are based on one Buddhist's experiences, from the point of view of a monastic with nearly thirty years of practice as a monk, as well as two decades of pastoral service to lay communities both in Asia and in the West.

Fasting in the monastic community is considered an ascetic practice, a *dhutanga* practice. (*Dhutanga* means "to shake up" or "invigorate.") *Dhutangas* are a specific list of thirteen practices, four of which pertain to food: eating once a day; eating at one sitting; reducing the amount you eat; and on alms-round, eating only the food that you receive at the first seven houses. These practices are adopted by individuals voluntarily—they are not required in the normal course of a Buddhist monastic's life of practice. The Buddha, as is well known, emphasized moderation, the middle way that avoids extremes, in all things. Fasting is an additional method that one can take up, with supervision, for a time.

How did the Buddha's own experience influence the Buddhist approach to fasting?

The Buddha's spiritual awakening is directly related to fasting, but from the reverse. That is to say, only after the Buddha stopped fasting did he realize his *mahabodhi*, or great awakening. The founding story of the Buddhist faith relates how the Buddha was cultivating the way in the Himalayas, having left his affluent life as a prince of India. He sought teachers and investigated a variety of practices in his search for liberation from the suffering of old age, death, and rebirth. In the course of his practices, he realized that desire was the root of mortality. He determined, incorrectly, that if he stopped eating he could end desire and gain liberation from suffering. As the story goes, he ate only a grain of rice and a sesame seed per day. Over time he got so thin that he could touch his spine by pressing on his stomach. He no longer had the strength to meditate. He realized that he would die before he understood his mind; further, that desire does not end by force. At that point, a young herdsmaid offered him a meal of milk porridge, which he accepted. He regained his strength, renewed his meditation, and realized Buddhahood. So by quitting fasting and eating in moderation, he realized the central tenet of Buddhist practice—moderation.

In Buddhism, who fasts? Are there any exemptions due to age? For example, do children fast? Do adults over a certain age not fast?

Fasting in the lay community in Asia is typified by the Chinese word *zhai* or *zai,* which means at the same time "vegetarian" as well as "fasting." The point is that removing the meat from your diet, twice a month on the new or full moon days, or six times a month, or more often, is often considered already a kind of fasting. The principle holds that removing indulgences from the diet, in this case, nutrients that are luxuries eaten to satisfy the desire for flavor, is already a form of fasting, and brings merit to the one who fasts.

For monastics, it's a different story. Fasting, because it is a difficult practice, is undertaken with supervision, under the guidance of a skilled mentor. Children rarely fast in any method connected with the Buddhist religion.

What does a fast day look like? For instance, are some foods permitted but not others? Some drinks but not others? Or is it a complete abstinence from all food and all drink?

When a practitioner adopts a supervised fasting practice, he or she eats dry bread for three days to prepare the stomach for no food. The standard fasting period is eighteen days, and only a small amount of water is drunk daily. Most important is the ending of the fast, which requires small portions of thin porridge or gruel every few hours for three days, until the digestive system has come fully back to life. If this first fast is successful and beneficial to your practice, then you can attempt a thirty-six day fast. Some fasters have extended the period gradually over years to include fasting for up to seventy-two days. This is an extreme practice that is only recommended if you have taken all the required steps with the supervision of an experienced teacher.

What part does fasting play in the life of the average Buddhist? How long would a normal fast be?

To understand how Mahayana Buddhists practice fasting, it helps to understand their daily practices regarding food. Many Buddhists are vegetarians, but not all, by any means. This comes as a surprise to many people who assume that Buddhists, being motivated by great compassion, would not eat the flesh of living beings. This issue has traditionally provoked debate among Buddhists. Chinese and Vietnamese Buddhists from the Mahayana or northern tradition are strict vegetarians. This tradition avoids the five pungent plants (onions, garlic, shallots, leeks, and chives) as well as eggs, and of course alcohol and tobacco in any form.

Avoiding dairy and following a vegan diet is a personal option and not a requirement. Some Buddhists eat only once per day, before noon. This practice accords with an account in *The Sutra in Forty-Two Sections,* a Mahayana scripture, which relates how the Buddha ate one meal a day, before noon.

To those who are not monks—and maybe even to some of those who are—this may look like extreme asceticism. Presumably the emphasis on moderation finds more evident expression in the lives of nonmonastics. Where, for example, would fasting fit into the world of lay Buddhists who have families and jobs?

Folks who function in the world of the marketplace need sufficient nutrition to carry on their various affairs. Certainly, overeating and undereating both defeat the purpose of food, which is to nourish the body and keep us healthy so that we can work to benefit the world.

Would the practice of fasting be different among vowed members within the tradition?

Laity who receive and observe the vows, known as the lay bodhisattva precepts, stop eating at noon on six days of each month. The purpose of their limiting food intake is manifold: out of compassion for those suffering from starvation, they "give by reducing their share." Further, they respect the Buddha's practice of moderation and eat less on those days. The fasting observance is related to several liturgical practices observed on the six fasting days: They recite their precept codes, recite scriptures, and increase their hours of meditation on those days.

For what reasons would Buddhists fast? Would one motivating reason tend to play a more significant role than others?

Some Buddhist laity feel that eating low on the food chain creates merit; eating less luxurious food creates an opportunity to serve the planet and all living beings. In this way, the dining table becomes a place of practice.

Buddhist monastics who adopt the fasting practice described above do so by and large to purify their bodies and to clarify their thoughts. Fasting allows coarse thoughts to diminish, but strength also diminishes, so there is a tradeoff between mental clarity and reduced ability to meditate as long. Some monastics report that the longer they fast, the more strength they have, so not everybody's experience is the same.

The Buddha's own experience showed him that fasting per se did not extinguish desire, it only subdued it. As soon as he resumed eating, his desire returned as well. It took concentration and insight to extinguish desire. The Buddha discovered that desire is rooted in the mind and can be transformed in the mind. Fasting can help that process of transforming desire to wisdom by subduing the body's coarse desires. Fasting is an aid to the way, a supplementary practice that can lead to increased mental awareness of the connection between desire and human existence.

Moreover fasting highlights your attachments to food and to good flavor; thus it helps you to distinguish how much of your craving for food is need, and therefore normal and necessary, and how much is greed, and therefore a hindrance to liberation.

Is fasting related at all to almsgiving in general practice?
Monks from the Theravada tradition hold that it is necessary to accept without exception whatever the lay donors put in their alms bowls. If the donation includes meat, many Theravada monks will eat it, regardless. Mahayana monks and nuns feel that compassion should be the priority, and it is a monk's duty to inform the laity that meat eating breaks the precept against killing. Killing obviously involves suffering in the animal killed for food; at the same time, it harms the seeds of compassion in the heart of the one who kills or eats the animal's body. This principle informs the monastic's approach toward the alms that he or she accepts from laity.

What significance does fasting hold for you personally?

I observed an eighteen-day fast and was not particularly successful. My constitution tends toward *pitta,* or "fire," in the Indian Ayurvedic scheme, and fasting makes my internal fire balance go over the top. Eating just enough, every day, of wholesome vegetarian food seems to be the best balance for me.

CHAPTER SEVEN

LATTER-DAY SAINTS: OFFERINGS FOR THOSE IN WANT, STRENGTHENING IN THE FAITH

In the spring of 1820, a fourteen-year-old boy named Joseph Smith went into a grove of trees near his home in Palmyra, New York, and prayed to learn which church he should join. He learned in a vision that the church of Christ, due to apostasy among Jesus's followers, no longer existed on earth and that he was chosen by God to restore it. During the next ten years, visited by other heavenly messengers, Smith translated the Book of Mormon and received authority to organize the Church of Jesus Christ of Latter-day Saints, which was formally instituted in April 1830 under his leadership.

The Book of Mormon is seen as another witness of Jesus Christ. In Mormon understanding, it contains the writings of ancient prophets. One of these, Lehi, lived in Jerusalem around 600 BCE. God commanded Lehi to lead a small group of people to the American continent. There they became a great civilization. God continued to call prophets among these people. The Book of Mormon is a collection of the writings of these prophets and record keepers. It is named after Mormon, one of the last of these ancient prophets. These prophets knew about God's plan and the mission of Jesus Christ. They recorded that Christ appeared, after his resurrection, to the people in America, taught them his gospel, and formed his church among them. The book contains teachings of Christ, and it supports and verifies the Bible. In addition to translating the Book of Mormon, Joseph Smith recorded other revelations he received from God. Many of these revelations are found in two books of modern-day scripture: *Doctrine and Covenants* and *The Pearl of Great Price.*

The priesthood, reestablished under Joseph Smith, has two divisions. The lesser priesthood is called the Aaronic priesthood, named after Aaron in the Hebrew Bible. It includes the authority to preach the gospel of repentance and to baptize. The greater priesthood is called the Melchizedek priesthood, named after Melchizedek in the Hebrew Bible. It includes the authority to preside over the church and to perform all ordinances. All male members who are prepared receive the priesthood to help lead the church.

The current prophet-successor to Joseph Smith and president of the Church of Jesus Christ of Latter-day Saints, Gordon B. Hinckley, is assisted by two counselors; together, they make up the First Presidency of the church. With twelve others, referred to as the Quorum of the Twelve Apostles, they lead the church, which is understood not as a Reformation church, but as a Restoration. Those who are among the Quorum of the Twelve, as well as those who hold the Melchizedek priesthood and men who are on missions, bear the title of Elder.

This brief background will be helpful in understanding some of the references that follow in our consideration of fasting in the lives of Latter-day Saints (LDS).

THE ORDINANCE TO FAST

In a revelation to the prophet Joseph Smith, the Lord commanded the Latter-day Saints to "continue in prayer and fasting from this time forth" (*Doctrine and Covenants* 88:76). In the early twentieth century, one of the prophet's namesakes, Sixth Church President Joseph F. Smith, gave further qualification to this ordinance when he said fasting "is a duty from which we cannot escape; but let it be remembered that the observance of this fast day by abstaining 24 hours from food and drink is not an absolute rule ... but it is left with the people as a matter of conscience, to exercise wisdom and discretion."[1] Those with health problems that preclude fasting, pregnant women, mothers nursing children, and those too young to understand the purpose of fasting are not to feel compelled to fast.

Church members are encouraged to fast regularly once each month on fast day and also whenever their faith needs special strengthening. The fast contemplated on the day referred to as "fast day" is that food and drink are not to be taken for twenty-four hours, "from even to even" as defined by President Smith. "From even to even" has been given the meaning of going without two meals from the evening meal on the night before to the evening meal on fast day. Members who are physically able are encouraged to fast, pray, bear witness to the truthfulness of the gospel, and contribute a generous fast offering to help the poor. The offering should be at least equal to the value of the food that would have been eaten. Typically, the first Sunday of each month is designated as fast Sunday.[2]

In addition, an individual, a family, or a congregation may fast for a specific cause, such as praying for the recovery of a sick friend, resolving doubts, or accepting a new calling. When preparing for a difficult task or a life change, one person may simply desire to spend some intimate time in prayer, making fasting an integral part of the day. Another person may fast when seeking strength to overcome weakness, to endure trial, to express grief, or to find spiritual enlightenment or guidance in decision making.

EVOLUTION OF THE MONTHLY FAST DAY

LDS Elder Howard Hunter of the Quorum of the Twelve Apostles relates the evolution of a communal fast day in the life of the church.[3] Modern revelation as contained in the *Doctrine and Covenants* makes little mention of fasting and gives no specific instructions regarding it. A year and a half after the church was organized, the prophet Joseph Smith received a revelation that mentions observance of the Lord's day and incidentally refers to fasting, without commenting further on it.

> And on this day thou shalt do none other thing, only let thy food be prepared with singleness of heart that thy fasting may be perfect, or, in other words, that thy joy may be full. Verily, this is fasting and prayer, or in other words, rejoicing and prayer. (*Doctrine and Covenants* 59:13–14)

The following year there came the more explicit revelation from the Lord on the subject to which we alluded above: "I give unto you a commandment that ye shall continue in prayer and fasting from this time forth" (*Doctrine and Covenants* 88:76). Before this, there had been no observance of a fast in the church on any regular basis. The wording seems to suggest the institution of fast meetings, but there is no evidence that any took place until the first temple was built in Kirtland, Ohio, in 1836. It is not known when fasting was adopted in the church as a regular observance, but there are records that indicate that some meetings in which people were fasting were held in the Kirtland Temple on the first Thursday of each month in 1836. There is, however, no indication that these fasts were associated with donations to the poor, except a remark made by Brigham Young more than thirty years later in Salt Lake City:

You know that the first Thursday in each month we hold as a fast day. How many here know the origin of this day? Before tithing was paid, the poor were supported by donations. They came to Joseph [Smith] and wanted help, in Kirtland, and he said there should be a fast day, which was decided upon. It was to be held once a month, as it is now, and all that would have been eaten that day, of flour, or meat, or butter, or fruit, or anything else, was to be carried to the fast meeting and put into the hands of a person selected for the purpose of taking care of it and distributing it among the poor. (*Journal of Discourses,* 12:115)

Although Brigham Young indicated that there was a decision made, there is no record that it was ever observed. But after the Saints arrived in the Salt Lake Valley in Utah, a prolonged period of drought, an exceptionally hard winter, and a plague of grasshoppers in 1855–1856 resulted in desperate circumstances. To meet the great demands of dire need within the community in those trying years, a fast day on the first Thursday of every month did come into existence. What was not eaten by those fasting was gathered up and given to those in want. The convention for meeting that emergency became an established institution. Before this time, the poor had been sustained by donations, but now the care of the needy became directly related to the fast day. What was donated became known as "fast offerings," brought to the monthly fast meetings.

When the membership of the church was still small, the holding of the fast day on Thursday proved workable. But as time went on and the membership grew, difficulties emerged: Employees had to take time from their work and merchants had to close their businesses. So a decision was made by the First Presidency and the Twelve that the monthly fast meeting should be held on the first Sunday of each month. The first Sunday of

December 1896 was the date set for the change, and from that time to the present, the fast day has been observed on the first Sunday of the month.

FAST OFFERINGS FOR THE POOR

"The law of the fast has three great purposes," writes Elder L. Tom Perry of the Quorum of the Twelve Apostles. "First, it provides assistance to the needy through the contribution of fast offerings, consisting of the value of meals from which we abstain. Second, a fast is beneficial to us physically. Third, it is to increase humility and spirituality on the part of each individual."[4] The primacy of assistance to the needy over all other values derives from scriptural mandate as well as historical exigency.

In the Book of Mormon, King Benjamin addressed the people in these terms:

> And now, for the sake of these things which I have spoken unto you—that is for the sake of retaining a remission of your sins from day to day, that ye may walk guiltless before God—I would that ye should impart of your substance to the poor, every man according to that which he hath, such as feeding the hungry, clothing the naked, visiting the sick, and administering to their relief, both spiritually and temporally, according to their wants. (Mosiah 4:26)

Another Book of Mormon prophet, Amulek, explained that often prayers have no power because those who offer them have turned their backs on the needy. The concept of fast offerings in LDS practice for those in want finds reference as well to the admonition of Isaiah, the prophet in the Hebrew scriptures, to "share your bread with the hungry" (Isa. 58:7) and to the postapostolic New Testament church in which several early Christian fathers like St. Augustine, St. John Chrysostom, and

St. Peter Chrysologus preached that a fast that did not somehow benefit others fell short. In LDS understanding, this biblical and historical emphasis has been restored and given concrete expression in our day by the Lord through the prophet Joseph Smith.

We have seen how the prophet instituted the practice of collecting fast offerings for the poor in Kirtland, where LDS members had begun gathering in the early 1830s. Later, in Nauvoo, Illinois, in 1845, the Quorum of the Twelve Apostles sent a general letter to the church defining the "principles of fasts," stating:

> Let this be an example to all saints, and there will never be any lack for bread: When the poor are starving, let those who have, fast one day and give what they otherwise would have eaten to the bishops for the poor, and everyone will abound for a long time; and this is one great and important principle of fasts approved of the Lord.[5]

At that time, in a pioneer economy, most donations were of food and livestock. Today, fast offerings usually consist of cash collected by Aaronic priesthood deacons, who often serve as agents of the bishop in collecting fast donations. Wards and stakes (similar to dioceses and parishes) are encouraged to be self-reliant in providing for the needs of the poor in their area. Whatever is not used locally is forwarded to LDS national headquarters and redistributed to areas of greatest need. Historically, though, fast offerings have seldom been sufficient to provide for all the welfare needs of the church, and shortages have been met from general church funds.[6]

KEEPING THE SPIRIT OF THE FAST ALIVE

Those Saints who fast are counseled to follow these steps:

- Pray before beginning your fast.
- Fast with a purpose, and think often about the purpose of your fast.

- Remain cheerful and patient.
- Offer a prayer of gratitude at the end of your fast.

Prayer is a necessary part of fasting. Without it, fasting is not complete; it is simply going hungry. Throughout the scriptures prayer and fasting are mentioned in the same breath. Fasting with prayer as its companion fosters a spirit of devotion and love of God. It increases faith in your heart, encourages humility and contrition of soul, teaches you about your dependence on God, and draws you further along the path to salvation. Thus every fast should begin and end with prayer.[7] As one church elder expressed it, "If we want our fasting to be more than just going without eating, we must lift our hearts, our minds, and our voices in communion with our Heavenly Father. Fast, coupled with mighty prayer, is powerful. It can fill our minds with the revelations of the Spirit."[8]

Fasting can have many purposes, but it is important to be clear with yourself about what that purpose is and keep it focused throughout the day by returning to it frequently in order to sustain your motivation from the beginning to the end. One of its promised fruits is that the person fasting will experience a quiet joy within since the closer you feel to the Lord, the greater is your joy. Learning to embrace the sacrifice involved with a cheerful spirit contributes to strength of character. That reason alone makes fasting important. More than just the control of your physical appetite is involved—it is the control of your passions and temper as well.

FAST AND TESTIMONY MEETINGS

An LDS fast and testimony meeting is normally held on the first Sunday of each month. A member of the bishopric or branch presidency conducts the meeting, where members of the church partake of the sacrament of the Lord's Supper. After the sacrament has been administered, the person conducting the meeting expresses his or her testimony, then invites the members of the congregation of all ages to bear verbal witness to their experiences in trying to live the gospel of Jesus Christ as a way of strengthening themselves and one another.

The pulpit is open to anyone who wants to give a spontaneous short testimony. In the words of an acquaintance of mine who is a lifetime church member, "It can be alternately inspiring, amusing, and cringe-inducing, all in the same service." Because the individual expressions are rarely longer than five or six minutes, children and adults alike come forward or simply stand in place to speak. In any given year, a majority of the membership of the church, young and old, will have participated in giving witness.

> In this setting feelings of profoundest concern are often expressed: appreciation of good family relationships, thanksgiving for the blessings of the gospel, recognition of significant changes in lives, and the fruits of obedience. A faith-promoting experience may be shared or a witness given regarding a point of doctrine or attesting divine inspiration. Such expressions are usually concluded by a prayer or petition in the name of the Lord. The experience is at once enlightening, sobering, and moving. Tears are not uncommon amid acknowledgement of weaknesses and efforts to improve, along with gratitude for divine goodness.[9]

A LIVING VOICE FROM THE TRADITION

Sheryl Condie Kempton is a wife, mother, and writer. She describes here her efforts to make fasting a more meaningful practice in her life and some of the fruits it has borne.

A year ago I decided it was time for me to get back into the pattern of regular fasting. With my new resolve, I also wanted to try to learn how to make my fasts more meaningful: more acceptable to the Lord and more powerful in expanding my own spirituality.

Fast Sunday came. I intended to fast from Saturday afternoon until after fast and testimony meeting on Sunday afternoon—but on Saturday evening I attended a meeting where refreshments were served. I changed my plan: I would fast from late Saturday to late Sunday.

The next morning, amid the hurried atmosphere of trying to get my three little girls fed and ready for Sunday School, I suddenly caught myself licking dripped honey off my fingers and popping rejected bread crusts into my mouth. When I realized what I was doing, I felt discouraged and weak, and I gave up fasting that day.

I resolved to fast sometime later in the week to make up for my failure; but the week—and the month—passed without my accomplishing the goal. And so fast Sunday approached again.

This time things were different. [Then] President Spencer W. Kimball asked us to fast and pray about the weather situation, the bitter cold and snow in some areas and the drought in others. It was an inspiring feeling to know that I was joining hundreds of thousands of people in doing what a prophet of God asked, and that feeling motivated me to succeed.

But even though I did not eat or drink for 24 hours, I was not really satisfied with my effort. The day hadn't been much different from most Sundays, and it seemed to me that if fasting were important, it should make a difference. I knew that it was important, so I concluded that I must not be doing it right.

I decided to study the scriptures concerning the principles and practices of fasting.... I became more concerned that I was doing something wrong in my fasting. My fast Sundays had not been days particularly full of joy: At best, they were as joyful as any other Sunday; at worst, they were sometimes characterized by grouchiness, hunger, impatience, and bad feelings. And fast Sundays certainly did not produce a fullness of joy radiating through the rest of the month. For me, there was no noticeable difference between months when I fasted and months when I didn't. At that point I knew I was missing something that had made a profound difference in the lives of others....

With this information and an intense desire to do what was right, I was ready to experiment upon the words I had studied. I knew the law of the fast, and I knew that I could observe the outward letter of the law. But it is the spirit of the law that can really change our lives. I decided to focus on the following five areas in trying to obtain the spirit of fasting:

1. A spirit of love for God and for my fellow beings. These two most important goals need constant work and attention. Not only is it difficult for me to love some people some of the time, but it is also sometimes difficult to want to love them. And when I think of loving God, I am overwhelmed to know that even my best love at this point is a weak and meager gift.

2. A spirit of sacrifice and service. Fast offerings are one sign of this spirit. Another is a willingness to share my testimony with others. I must also diligently seek other opportunities to give and to share my abundance of blessings with others. Sometimes I feel that I don't even begin to understand what real sacrifice is.

3. A spirit of brotherhood and fellowship with the saints. It gives me a wonderful feeling of joy to realize, when I fast, that I am joining the rest of the church membership in this opportunity, and that we can gain power through unity.

4. A spirit of communion with God. For one day in each month I have an opportunity to put aside all distractions (except my three children, who cannot yet fully support me in my effort) and with "simplicity of intention" try to purify my heart to be one with God as I purify my body temple.

5. A spirit of self-control. To me, the exercise of my will in fasting is a sign of humility that I submit my will to the Lord's will, that I desire to strengthen my spiritual power and bodily discipline, and that I am willing to repent of wanting to do or doing other than what the Lord would desire.

With all this in mind, I fasted. The first time I fasted and prayed that I might withstand a particular temptation that had been bothering me. The results were miraculous. Not only did I withstand the temptation, but it ceased to be a temptation! Not only did I resist the sin, but I did not want to sin. And so I was immediately blessed.

I decided that it was important to my growth to fast again soon, and not wait for a whole month. This time I fasted and prayed about a decision I was having difficulty making. The pros and cons of the major alternatives seemed nearly equal, and I had been puzzling about it for several weeks. After fasting and praying about it, I suddenly knew what to do, and there was never another moment of wondering if it was the best choice. It is difficult to explain to anyone else the instant clearing of the cloudiness in my mind....

Since that time I have attempted to make fast Sunday be what I have learned it should be. This has brought real changes into my life, some of them quite surprising. For example, I noticed that after fasting I was not as competitive.... Another surprising result is that after fasting I was intensely aware of what food I put into my mouth. Somehow my body seemed more sacred to me; and I did not want to eat anything that was impure or unnecessary. It almost seems as if fasting can help us sense what foods are really nourishing to us, and which ones pollute our physical system.... I was more able to concentrate with singleness of purpose when I went to the temple.... I also felt an increased tenderness toward my husband and children.... I was more emotionally and spiritually receptive.... Another important blessing I have received as a result of fasting is an increased ability to recognize evil influences and temptations—and to dismiss them without consideration....

As I have renewed my efforts to fast as the Lord would have me do, I have discovered some practical aids to help me.

1. Be united in fasting as a family. Take strength and motivation from the priesthood example and support each other in the effort. Those who are not yet old enough to abstain from eating and drinking can still participate in the spirit: praying, learning scripture stories, singing, counting blessings, planning service to others.

2. Plan specific service and sacrifice for others. Always give a generous fast offering and seek inspiration concerning other service the Lord desires. "Undo the heavy burdens ... let the oppressed go free.... Deal thy bread to the hungry.... bring the poor ... to thy house. Cover the naked" (Isa. 58:6–7).

3. Prepare carefully so that physical work can be held to a minimum. For me, this means planning in advance what the children will wear and what they will eat. I also try to prepare appropriate Sunday activities for them before my fast begins on Saturday.

4. Prepare carefully so that my patience is not strained. Allow plenty of time to get ready for church meetings so that we don't need to hurry.

5. Plan time for intense prayer....

6. Fast and pray for a specific purpose or blessing. This might be a personal need, a family problem, a blessing for someone else, or something involving the whole church or country....

7. Repent of sins. Seek strength to change and inspiration on how to change. Seek ways to make restitution and to receive forgiveness from those I have wronged.

8. Read, study, and ponder the scriptures....

9. Praise God. Show gratitude for his blessings. Sing hymns of praise to him. Rejoice in my relationship with him. Bear testimony of him and his goodness to others.

10. Avoid social conflicts and distractions. Saturday night wedding receptions, parties, dinners, sports, and Sunday dinners may not contribute to fasting and spiritual communion....

11. Record my experiences in my journal. Include praise to God, what I repent of and my plans for change, commentary on the scriptures I have read, service I plan to do, the purposes for which I fast each month, and my testimony....

Even though my fasting still cannot perfectly be called "rejoicing and prayer," I feel much closer to that ideal than I did a year ago. I am grateful that I know that God lives, that we are his children, and that his desire for us is that we find joy. And now I'm convinced that fasting is an integral part of that joy. It is a crucial element in our effort to eliminate every weakness, strengthen every talent, become perfect so that we can rejoin our Father in heaven. I am thankful to him for revealing fasting as a powerful tool that can help us find our way back to him.[10]

WHAT MAKES FASTING A SACRED ART?

THE HINGE VIRTUES

The medieval Christian era identified four basic virtues as the cornerstones for every other conceivable virtue. They are prudence, fortitude, temperance, and justice. They have been called "the cardinal virtues," from the Latin word *cardo,* meaning "hinge." They are the four heavy-duty hinges from which all moral virtues hang.

The practice of fasting involves something from each of them. *Prudence* is the power of good judgment. This judgment is amply demonstrated in the moderating influences of each religious tradition in its practice. We are endowed with a mind and will capable of comprehending and putting to use our natural and in-built resources for health and healing. To do so, we must exercise good judgment.

Fortitude is the capacity to act courageously, to endure difficulty. Let's face it: It takes courage to swim upstream against the current of our societal myth that "more is better," to take the road less traveled, the one that veers away from self-indulgence.

And there are days when holding to our fast is downright difficult and takes real sacrifice.

Temperance means moderation in all our activities, a balanced approach. Where food is concerned: a proper, balanced
diet. Eating just what we need and learning to leave the table
before we're stuffed. A regular fast day for reattunement with
our Creator and ourselves. All these represent temperance in
action.

Justice is the virtue of rendering to everyone what is his
or her due. This virtue emerged clearly in the fasting practice
of each religion as one leg of the traditional prayer-fasting-
almsgiving tripod.

We will examine the last two hinge virtues more closely
here.

TEMPERANCE

When we look at fasting in the different religious traditions of
the world, certain values underlying the practice emerge as commonly acknowledged and shared—values such as attunement to
God, penance, physical and mental purification, self-restraint,
social solidarity.

A value that has not been frequently mentioned but that I
believe is implicitly manifest in the variety of approaches to fasting that we have seen is temperance, or moderation. Have you
noticed, for example, that none of the religions are proposing
anything extreme? Jews have two twenty-five-hour fasts and
five dawn-to-dusk fasts in the course of a year. In the Catholic
approach, while meat is forbidden, two small meals and one regular meal are allowed. The average length of a Muslim fast day
in Ramadan is 13.5 hours. In Hinduism and Buddhism, fasting
is totally up to the individual, but usually it means abstaining
from solid foods for no more than one day with some liquids
permitted. For Latter-day Saints, it's missing two meals once a
month. In the deep and innate wisdom expressed in the moder-

ation that characterizes the approach of every religion to fasting, there is a wider application for our living.

A father of three remarked to me that he was having difficulty interesting his youngest daughter in accompanying the family to church. "Why should I do that?" she said. "That's no fun." The father's reflection was that "our society is raising a generation of pleasure junkies where the questions that matter most are 'Is it fun?' or 'Will it feel good?'" But let's admit it: The child has a point. The place and meaning of pleasure in our lives *is* an important preliminary consideration, especially when dealing with a subject like fasting that may have first-level negative associations with unpleasantness. What those who try fasting are surprised to learn is that there is a deep and abiding sense of pleasure in it—the pleasure that comes from both feeling remarkably healthy and sensing a growing intimacy with God. There is, in fact, an immense pleasure in a balanced and centered life.

Temperance is not the puritanical enemy of pleasure; its goal is not repression or inhibition. It does not frown on all that is attractive in life. Rather than attacking sense pleasures, it guarantees them. It is a good habit proclaiming present and past mastery of reason; it protects as well as predicts the humanity of future actions. It is interested in safeguarding the happy medium of reason, which is the absolutely essential condition for peace and progress in human life. It insists on the full freedom that can be given only by intelligent control.

A friend of mine, Michael, directs a center for emotionally disturbed children. When he feels that a certain delicate inner focus is becoming blurred, he tempers the bombardment of stimuli with fasting. It's a form of temperance in his life:

> When my life is going too fast, I tend to be mentally all over the place, and not sensitive enough to the person or event that is present right now. When I fast, I listen better,

I'm clearer in what I say—perhaps because it's more peaceful inside myself. Fasting represents for me a respite from the over-stimulations of life, whether it be from auditory, visual, or food sources.

I fast to pull the loose threads together in my life— it's a movement within. When I'm in touch with what's within, I find I'm in tune with what's without. As I've been fasting periodically during the past several years, I've realized that it works on more levels than one, and I find that all the aspects of my life just flow better.

For Michael, fasting is like the fine-tuning knob on a stereo, enabling him to receive the signals being transmitted in his direction with greater clarity and to give clearer messages himself. A day characterized by such communication is a satisfying day. Such satisfaction, found amid the rigors of our work, is a deep and quiet pleasure—a pleasure born of temperance.

The spiritual seeker's critical question is not the legitimacy of pleasure or enjoyment, but rather the coordination of pleasure with the other goals of human life. It is precisely here that we must come to grips with a fundamental principle of human experience: Limitation is essential for the integration of the personality. This is the birthplace of temperance as a virtue. Pleasure must be limited if it is to be enjoyed. Limitation means that pleasure must be seen in the context of our whole life project. Limitation of any kind is too often seen as stunting, stifling, and dehumanizing.

The athlete in training is not inhuman because she limits her social engagements. The invalid recovering from a severe fever is not condemning food when he abstains from corned beef and cabbage. The monk dedicated to contemplation has an entirely different diet than the brawny bricklayer.

Temperance is not empty-headed. It is filled with common sense. It is a quality of beauty because the very essence of beauty is proportion. And temperance has as its striking note precisely that of moderation, of order, of proportion. It has an air of tranquility about it, like the beauty of a calm sea, a Vermont valley farm seen from a mountaintop, or a child's face immediately after a bath. Temperance is an intensely personal virtue, as beauty is an intensely personal thing. Yet it is a constant inspiration to others, as beauty always is. It is the refreshing touch of the breath of God's order.

I don't think anyone who has ever given him- or herself over to the unbridled pursuit of pleasure in an undisciplined life found that it delivered the kind of fulfillment promised or sought. There is a quality to the presence of a genuinely virtuous person that fascinates, invites, and challenges. The truth is that a genuinely virtuous life is both immensely attractive and has a rich yield of what we are all looking for: inner peace and a deep, abiding joy.

JUSTICE

Believers of all living faiths choose the patterns of prayer, fasting, and caring behavior for others in their quest for fulfillment. Through the ages, with the goading of scriptural witness and prophetic challenge, it has come to be accepted that fasting must be characterized by a radical turning to God with a corresponding openness to loving and serving our neighbor. If these two elements are lacking, fasting may have some beneficial effects physiologically and emotionally, but it will not be a true religious act.

When, through fasting, we let go of some of that independent control we strive to extend over our lives and resources, we move on to a different level of consciousness and a deeper sense of solidarity with every human being. In the experience of creaturely poverty that fasting brings, there is a sense of gentleness and kinship with every being that exists.

When we contemplate who God is and who we are, when we realize the utter gratuity of all creation, a profound thanksgiving wells up from the very depths of our being. All is gift, and gratefully received. Greed fades. Nothing is taken for granted. All is reverenced. There is a loving care for every person and every thing. Sufficiency is more than enough, for it is more than is deserved. It is what is wanted for all. And what we have is shared with that end in view. It is staggering to realize how much we have while others struggle just to survive. Environmental scientists calculate that North Americans' consumption of the earth's resources is double that of Europeans' and seven times that of Asians and Africans. With compassion and sensitivity, we must constantly be involved in justice-serving behavior.

This newfound consciousness renders us particularly sensitive to the physical, psychic, and spiritual needs of our fellow human beings. It becomes, for example, more and more difficult to eat and drink excessively knowing that others are looking in trash barrels or garbage dumps for something to put in their stomachs. Lanza del Vasto, one of Gandhi's disciples, once wrote: "When you think of men starving in the world you are forced to cry out for them with a more sensitive heart. One who fasts is made transparent. Others appear to him transparent. Their sufferings enter into him and he is without defense against them."

Fasting is a way of identifying with all the suffering peoples of the world, especially those dying of hunger. We tend to forget the pain of the world if we are always very comfortable.

Through the centuries fasting has been used to draw communities of people together, providing them with a common experience and the opportunity to share that experience: Lent, the Day of Atonement, Ramadan, the fast Sunday. Fasting has also been used to organize groups around social change movements. Many leaders of such groups have fasted as an act of exemplary sacrifice and discipline, often dramatizing an issue and bringing it to public attention. Mahatma Gandhi was a major practitioner of this approach through his fasts for Indian independence.

Gandhi's example has been a profound inspiration to other leaders of social reform in places as disparate as Sicily and California. In Sicily, Danilo Dolci rallied peasants around his fasts, inspiring them to throw off the yoke of oppression; in California, Cesar Chavez through his fasting example solidified the efforts of migrants to form a farmworkers' union.

Dramatic hunger strikes were used by many protestors during the civil rights movement and the Vietnam War and to protest nuclear power plants. These strikes can draw attention to a cause and often result in remedial action. Some see the remedial action merely in political terms. A fast carried on too long will cross the line into starvation and eventual death, and those at whom the fast is directed do not want to jeopardize their position further by creating a martyr. Others see the fast as a moral force, an effective instrument of spiritual intercession that cries out to God to change hearts. And still others see fasting as certainly possessing moral force but going beyond it to become an instrument of practical, concrete action. This last approach—the fast as a practical action—is where we, as citizens of a global village, can take responsibility for world hunger.

We see the development of new farming technologies, the worldwide network of transportation and communication. We know that enough food *can* be grown and *can* be distributed. What stops it from happening? To answer this question, representatives of 130 national governments assembled for the first time in Rome in 1974 under United Nations auspices for the World Food Conference. The conference proposed a world food-reserve program coordinated internationally, but with supplies held nationally. In order to coordinate this and other related proposals, the United Nations established the World Food Council, with headquarters in Rome. The conference examined the political nature of food distribution. It called for broad social and economic reforms in poor countries, including land and tax reforms that would benefit small farm holders and landless peasants, in order to noticeably reduce hunger. It asked for a new economic relationship between rich and poor countries to close the widening gap between them. This initiative points toward areas such as trade, investment, and the monetary system. Actions at this level are often the most important and difficult of all.

Analyzing hunger on an international scale makes us realize that we will not deal effectively with hunger simply through private acts of charity. It may be possible for us, for example, to feed a hungry family or two near us (something well worth doing) without altering the conditions that brought about their hunger. If we really care about hungry people, we must eventually ask *why* they are hungry. They are hungry because they are poor, which means we cannot come to terms with hunger unless we deal with poverty. We are then confronted with the harsh realities behind why some have and others have not. In the end, to make lasting gains against hunger, we must also demand justice.

The fact that 5 percent of the human race consumes more marketable wealth than does the poor 70 percent of the world has prompted many to reexamine their lifestyles and shift toward a more frugal, less consumerist way of life. Many religious traditions value simplicity; many ordinary people have chosen to embrace it. But the chief value in this lifestyle is spiritual and symbolic; it places you more fully at the disposal of God and other people and keeps a sense of proportion. Adopting a simpler lifestyle will not directly transfer resources to those in want. Similarly, going without food for one day a week and contributing to a good cause the money that you would otherwise have spent for your meals fails to go to the heart of the problem.

Furthermore, although lifestyle changes appeal as immediate, personal responses, they can also lull us into a false sense of fulfillment. Cutting down on our food intake and consumerist habits because most of the world's poor cannot afford to eat and live in the manner of North Americans may be morally satisfying, but unless it is accompanied by more positive steps, it may do nothing more on the practical level of feeding the hungry than put people out of work. It is like swinging at the ball but only nicking it, as opposed to hitting it squarely. To hit it squarely, we need to move from the personal to the public realm. Food will reach hungry people only if government policies see to its adequate production and distribution.

To the question "What can I do besides give?" the World Food Conference implicitly told the average citizen: "Influence government policy." That answer should not discourage giving on the personal, neighborhood, or city level, but it tells us that it is necessary to move beyond the adjusted-lifestyle approach if we are really interested in doing something about feeding the hungry. Adopting a more modest lifestyle can be a powerful witness in the struggle against hunger, if efforts to change public policy accompany it.

If, for instance, I use my lunch hour on a fast day to write a letter that tells my representative in Congress what I think of our public policy regarding food distribution and what I want our country to do, that kind of response to world hunger brings together lifestyle adjustment (my fast) with positive action (my letters) to influence government policy. Our sense of responsibility must become sufficiently deep to encompass both.

This effort to be all-encompassing can also challenge the charity-begins-at-home argument that says, "Shouldn't we eliminate hunger here before we try to solve the problem worldwide?" There's no need to pit domestic hunger against world hunger. We can deal with both.

The urgent need is not for faith communities *as faith communities* to enter the political fray but for believers *as citizens* to exercise their renewed consciences and contact decision makers, becoming a voice for the hungry to their government representatives. That is exactly what gave birth to the citizens' movement Bread for the World.

In 1972 a small group of Catholics and Protestants met to reflect on how people of faith could be mobilized to influence U.S. policies that address the causes of world hunger. Their small group has grown to a nationwide, nonpartisan citizens' movement of more than fifty thousand members whose work is supported by forty-five denominations—Roman Catholic, mainline Protestant, Evangelical, Pentecostal, and Orthodox— and whose board of directors includes grassroots leaders, members of Congress, and representatives of various charities. Many people of other faiths also join in their work. Bread for the World members are organized by congressional district into local networks nationwide. They write, call, and visit members of Congress and generate media attention about national legislation and other efforts that address hunger. These "Hunger Basics" are presented on the organization's website:

> More than 800 million people in the world go hungry.
>
> In developing countries, 6 million children die each year, mostly from hunger-related causes.
>
> In the United States, 13 million children live in households where people have to skip meals or eat less to make ends meet. That means one in ten households in the U.S. are living with hunger or are at risk of hunger.
>
> But we *can* end hunger.
>
> We have the means. The financial costs to end hunger are relatively slight. The United Nations Development Program estimates that the basic health and nutrition needs of the world's poorest people could be met for an additional $13 billion a year. Animal lovers in the United States and Europe spend more than that on pet food each year.

What makes the difference between millions of hungry people and a world where all are fed?

Only a change in priorities. Only the will to end
hunger.[1]

Bread for the World's research institute seeks justice for
hungry people by engaging in research and education on policies
relating to hunger and development. Available are Sunday
school resources, booklets with exercises, scripture passages,
prayers, and a "Leader's Guide" to help present important
hunger and poverty issues to congregation study groups. The
institute also serves as secretariat for the Alliance to End
Hunger, a coalition of religious bodies, foundations, labor
unions, corporate leaders, advocacy groups, civil rights groups,
and charitable organizations. The mission of the alliance is to
change public opinion and policy to significantly reduce hunger
in the United States and internationally.

A single action by Congress or Parliament, one decision by
the president or prime minister, can multiply—or undo—many
times over all our voluntary contributions derived from fast
days. To give to the poor is good, but it doesn't go far enough if
we leave the big decisions up to political representatives without
letting them know what we want. Our citizenship is our most
powerful tool against hunger. Not to exercise it is taken as indif-
ference when policies are being worked out; it leaves leaders free
to make decisions by other standards and results in hungry people becoming victims of political lobbying. Saying nothing to
political leaders *is* saying something to them. Ordinary people
can help the nation reach out to a hungry world. But to do so, we
will have to add to our contributions for those in want the offering of our political activism to influence government policy.

Ratcheting up our involvement in such practical terms is part
of what it means to "prepare to practice" fasting as a religious act.
A discipline of the spiritual life, if it is to be truly that, is always

about more than just yourself. The golden rule—do unto others as you would have them do unto you—is shared by every religion in the world. St. Augustine's words come to mind: "Your privations will be fruitful if you provide for the needs of another. Certainly you have deprived your body, but to whom did you give that which you deprived yourself? Fast, then, in such a way that when another has eaten in your place you may rejoice in the meal you have not taken. Then your offering will be received by God."

This reflection on the social responsibility dimension of fasting is a necessary counterweight to the next chapter, which discusses the personal health benefits of fasting. Both approaches —the social and the personal—have their place; each is anchored in one or the other of the cardinal, hinge virtues: prudence, fortitude, temperance, and justice. The challenge is to hold the personal and the social dimensions together. We can become so fascinated by and enamored of the sheer physiological process and benefits of fasting that it erases everything else from our minds and ends up being just something we do for our own personal health. Practicing fasting for personal cleansing alone drains the transcendent dimension out of it. This is a plea to keep in mind the distinctive nature of fasting as a religious act and as something done for, if not with, others as well as for yourself.

As the Muslim scholar Al-Ghazzali says, fasting, "like every act of worship is possessed of an outward and an inner secret, an external husk and an internal pith. The husks are of different grades and each grade has different layers. It is for you to choose whether to be content with the husk or join the company of the wise and learned."[2] What makes fasting an *art* is holding the husk and the pith, the outer form and the inner intention, together in harmonious balance. What makes it a *sacred* art is its motivating self-love and other-love, and God to whom it is offered in love.

CHAPTER NINE

PREPARING TO PRACTICE

Spirituality relates to the practical, affective, and transforma-
tive dimension of a religious tradition. This definition is
grounded in two convictions: First, that there are dimensions of
reality that are not immediately obvious; and second, that contact with these dimensions can heal personal alienation and
fragmentation.

Spiritual practices within a religious tradition are both pedagogical and transformational. They are pedagogical in that they
teach us how to become spiritual. A regular practice inculcates a
way of life through regular, committed disciplines. They are
transformational in that they help us to break away from inau-
thentic ways of living in order to embrace a more authentic way
through the power that comes from contact with a more radical
level of reality. This radical reorientation literally "trans-forms"
in that it moves us from one life pattern to another.

When you undergo a religious conversion, a movement of
transformation is precipitated. But you need regular spiritual

practices to sustain the initial reorientation. Regular practice provides the structures for deepening and expanding religious conversion. Spiritual practices such as prayer, fasting, and alms-giving are engaged in out of the conviction that it is God's inten-tion to form people distinguished by certain qualities of the heart. Regular practice shapes the affections and dispositions of the heart, which in turn leads to corresponding actions. A par-ticular practice has usually evolved over time and has a history and structure that supports the values involved in it. It is a rich and meaningful human activity that we engage in because it is good and it is worthwhile doing. Regular practice has a forma-tive effect on our character when done well because through it our relationship with God develops. Done over time, spiritual practices become habits, and those routines can be the matrix for the deep work of God's Spirit in us.[1]

FREQUENTLY ASKED QUESTIONS

The range of questions presented here is limited by virtue of the kind of fasting proposed—short fasts of twelve to twenty-five hours—by the different religions that have provided the param-eters of our discussion. For those who may not be aware, it is not unusual for people to enjoin water-only fasts of four to ten days, or juice fasts of four to thirty days.[2] Obviously, time frames like these evoke a broader range of questions. What is salutary about even knowing people do this is that it can serve to tame your fears in contemplating fasting within the moderate frameworks proposed by the respective religious communities.

IS IT SAFE TO FAST?

First of all, I want to honor the fear underneath the question. The ultimate fear—will I survive?—reflects honestly the con-frontation with our mortality, our neediness, our finitude, that occurs in fasting. One of the spiritual benefits of fasting is that it provides us with an opportunity to listen to what comes up within us, to fears that are generally repressed. When this happens, the best thing to do is to see where the fear comes from, acknowledge it, try to understand whatever meanings may be attached to it, and respond to it (which may mean just letting it go). This kind of deep inner listening is in part what fasting as a spiritual practice is all about.

Now, the material-level response: When we fast, we in effect decide that we are going to take our nourishment from the "reserves" we have been storing up in good supply. Starvation begins when the "storage shelves" have been emptied, when the body has consumed its spare resources, craves food, and continues to be deprived. The fasting stage continues so long as the body supports itself on the stored reserves within its tissues. Starvation begins when abstinence is carried beyond the time when these stored reserves are used up or have dropped to a dangerously low level. It takes a very long fast (generally beyond forty days) to cross the line into starvation.

When the body is not receiving the needed nutrition through new incoming food, particularly proteins and fats, it will burn and digest its own tissues by the process of autolysis, or self-digestion. The body, however, does not perform this process of autolysis indiscriminately. In its wisdom, the body will first decompose and burn those cells and tissues which are diseased, aged, damaged, or dead, and this is where fasting earns the reputation of being a curative and rejuvenative therapy. Simply stated, the body feeds itself on the most impure and inferior materials, such as dead cells and morbid accumulations and fat deposits. It is for this reason that fasting is sometimes called a refuse disposal or a burning of rubbish. Rest assured, however, that the essential tissues and vital organs, the glands, the nervous system, and the brain are not damaged or digested in short-term fasting.

At the same time these old cells and diseased tissues are decomposed and burned, the building of new, healthy cells is expedited. Fasting speeds up the elimination of dead and dying cells, as well as accelerates the building of new cells. The toxic waste products that interfere with the nourishment of the cells are effectively eliminated, and the normal metabolic rate and cell oxygenation are restored. The end result: The fast exerts a normalizing, stabilizing, and rejuvenative effect on all the vital physiological, nervous, and mental functions. The nervous system is rejuvenated, mental powers are improved, glandular chemistry and hormonal secretions are stimulated and increased, and the biochemical and mineral balance of the tissue is normalized.

Fasting *is* safe for almost everybody. (Those who are responsible for the "almost" in that sentence will be specified in the next question.)

SHOULD I SEE A DOCTOR?
Most people don't consult a doctor before starting to fast, any more than they do before starting a diet. But what have you got to lose? If you have a checkup before you fast, you're on the safe side. Most people can fast, although there are a few who, because of special conditions, should not:[3]

- Those who are or have been anorexic or bulimic
- Pregnant, diabetic women
- Nursing mothers
- Those who have severe anemia
- Those with porphyria (a genetic metabolic defect)
- Those with a rare, genetic fatty-acid deficiency that prevents proper ketosis (the use of fatty acids instead of glucose as fuel) from occurring

If you have any of the above conditions, a list of alternate ways of fasting that have nothing to do with abstinence from food is given at the end of this chapter.

The literature on the healing effects of fasting is extensive but generally presumes longer fasts than are discussed here. To cite but a brief and partial list, diseases that have responded to fasting are: type II diabetes, chronic cardiovascular disease, acute pancreatitis, osteoarthritis and rheumatoid arthritis, severe toxic contamination, psychosomatic disease, neurogenic bladder, psoriasis, eczema, thrombophlebitis, varicose ulcers, fibromyalgia, neurocirculatory disease, irritable bowel syndrome, inflammatory bowel disease, bronchial asthma, lumbago, depression, neurosis, schizophrenia, duodenal ulcers, uterine fibroids, intestinal parasites, gout, allergies, hay fever, hives, multiple sclerosis, and insomnia.[4]

You may have noticed in the preceding chapters that pregnant women and women who have just given birth are always exempt from fasting. However, for the record, short-term fasting during pregnancy for nondiabetic women has not been found harmful to either mother or fetus. Similarly, children and teenagers can fast without complications if the fasts are short.[5] They could also, however, participate in a fast by eating small balanced meals, giving up junk food, or doing something else that helps them feel they are sharing in the family or community fasting experience. If you are a "golden ager," make sure you have the blessings of your doctor. A person who has been taking drugs over a long period should fast only under medical supervision.

SHOULD I ALTER MY DAILY ROUTINE?

Perhaps the larger question here is: Why are you fasting? Be clear about that, and you may find the answer to this question. If the purpose of your fast is to cultivate God-consciousness, then you may even find yourself taking a day away from work and home and spending it at a retreat center or in the park. And if you decide or are obliged to carry on with your normal responsibilities, you will have some gaps in your day (mealtimes). *Be on your guard against the common pitfall here—to just stay at your tasks and get more work done.* Use this time to advance the spiritual dimension of your fast day by praying, reading the scriptures, writing in a journal, or taking a slow walk and opening yourself to honor the Creator in the wonders of creation. Should you, then, alter your routine when you fast? Definitely. The day is about reclaiming an intimacy with yourself and with God that does not characterize your nonfasting days, so doing some things differently is part of the program.

WHAT ABOUT EXERCISE?

An hour-long walk would be great. People's energy levels differ, of course, but in general, the healthy person who is fasting for twelve to twenty-five hours can continue with his or her usual exercise. Failure to exercise, in fact, may bring on fatigue. On the other hand, fasting represents a day of rest for your body-spirit, so a case can be made for cutting yourself some slack and, if you happen to be feeling tired, taking a nap if you can. You will instinctively know if you have to cut back a bit; your body will tell you if you're overdoing it. Besides exercising moderately, keep warm, get plenty of fresh air, and avoid hot baths and saunas because of their dehydrating effects.

SHOULD I CONTINUE TAKING VITAMINS AND MINERALS?

As regards vitamins, minerals, and other food supplements, some say discontinue, others say go ahead and keep on taking them if you want to. Dr. Stuart Hill, member of the Science Council of Canada, suggests that taking vitamins can lead to problems because they contain substances other than the specific vitamins. These substances (for example, the corn filler or covering of many vitamins) may trigger allergic reactions that are normally masked by other foods. Hence, the recommendation that one should not take vitamins, medication, or pills of any other kind without a doctor's approval.

WHAT ABOUT WEIGHT LOSS?

One usually loses one to two pounds a day, mainly in fat tissues, when fasting. This is easily gained back after the fast if it is part of your "ideal" weight. You will return to your normal weight very quickly if the fast has brought you below that.

Currently, nearly two-thirds of all adults and more than one in ten youths are considered overweight or obese.[6] We live in a toxic nutritional environment of our own making, and we're drowning in a sea of calories. The average dinner plate has grown 40 percent since the Second World War. Children growing up now are the first generation expected to have a shorter lifespan than their parents. The insurance companies have a new mantra: Eat less and exercise more.

We oftentimes think that increasing the quantity of food will give us more energy, when what actually happens is that we end up feeling enervated and listless. Overeating paralyzes us, and then we experience the need for something to "get us going," so we reach for stimulants: coffee, tea, and tobacco. People are not nourished in proportion to the amount of food they eat but in proportion to how much they digest and assimilate. Food and nutrition are not the same thing. The amount of food taken in is not the key to the state of nutrition; the key is how much food is digested and assimilated. When assimilation and digestion are malfunctioning, it is futile to stuff a lot of food into the body. It is precisely those systems that need to be rejuvenated.

Ironically, since fasting improves the metabolism, abstaining from food can help an underweight person gain weight in the long run by providing a period of physiological rest and helping the body to better digest and more effectively assimilate essential nutrients. Such a step should be done under medical supervision, however.

WHAT ABOUT PEOPLE WITH HEART PROBLEMS?

The United States holds the record: We lead the world in heart and artery problems. Every second of the day someone is dying of a heart attack. Heart trouble is one of the scourges of Western civilization. Yet, diseases of the heart do not build up rapidly. It takes a long time to harden and block an artery. There are many contributing causes: cholesterol, fats, and fibrous tissues are responsible for the blocking and obstructing of the arteries; lack of exercise also contributes to arterial degeneration. As the inner passage of the arteries becomes so narrow that not enough blood can flow through to properly nourish the heart muscle, coronary occlusion occurs. We are all as old as our arteries. Inasmuch as fasting cleanses internal impurities, it is preventive health care.

WHAT ARE SOME OF THE POSITIVE PHYSICAL EFFECTS?

The body is a microcosm of the earth. Just as a whole host of toxins are poisoning the earth's ecosystem, so it is with our individual physical bodies—specially challenged in our era in which previously unknown unique synthetic chemicals are being developed and tried out on us. Basically, fasting allows the body to rest, detoxify, and heal. Normally, in addition to digesting food, which is its biggest job, the body works to eliminate wastes, fight diseases, ward off sickness, replenish worn-out cells, and nourish the blood. When it is relieved of its biggest job, the digestion of food, the system can catch up on some of its "backwork" in those other areas. Fasting normalizes metabolism and brings a welcome physiological rest for the digestive tract and the central nervous system. While you are unloading some of your emotional and spiritual "toxins" on a fast day, your body is cleansing itself and healing parts that are ill. Some of the benefits to which people attest:

You feel healthier. The health-improvement claims that you find in the literature on fasting cover a wide range. Sufferers of such assorted ailments as constipation, hay fever, asthma, peptic ulcers, arthritis, and colitis witness that their symptoms were significantly alleviated or disappeared altogether after a fast. Yogis say fasting gives them increased agility and concentration. Those who suffer from hay fever find the pollen seasons easier to take with regular fasting. Some people report that, after a fast, their skin takes on a better color and texture; eyes clear up and become brighter.

You feel tranquil. We sometimes turn to eating because we're anxious. We don't really need the food, but eating distracts us and gives us something to do. Fasting can be restful.

You sleep better. Nearly half the U.S. population complains of difficulty in getting to sleep and staying asleep. Fasting, nature's tranquilizer, relaxes the nervous system and eases the anxieties that account for much sleeplessness. It's what's going on in the internal organs that often keeps us awake; if they're at rest, sleep is going to flow much more naturally. Insomnia is directly related to overeating, heartburn, bloating, acid indigestion. As a further bonus, when the body is operating more efficiently (as is the case when one fasts regularly), many people find they need less sleep.

You kick your addictions. Once our bodies have become clean through fasting, our physiological systems will do their best to reject poisons. It sets up an active resistance to any new poisons that try to enter. People who have tried to break their addictions to coffee, alcohol, tobacco, or drugs have found fasting a great help in kicking the habit. Fasting helps you develop a new relationship with your body. The body will tell you what foods it likes, wants, and needs.

You free up some time for deeper pursuits. Certainly, eating is meant to be one of life's chief joys—a celebration of taste, color, smell, and texture. When people sit down together, it should be an event that closes the door on routine and opens a new space and time in which the food that is passed from hand to hand becomes a symbol of deeper sharing among those around the table. It is meant to be a time when the art of conversation is learned, where laughter levels the anxieties of the day. The meal experience is meant to be more than just putting food into our bodies.

The sad truth for many moderns, however, is that it isn't. It's an on-the-run, catch-as-catch-can, put-some-fuel-in-the-tank-to-keep-yourself-going experience. It often becomes, unfortunately, sheer pragmatics, as is witnessed by the tremendous number of people sitting alone and staring out the window at passersby from the stools and chairs of fast-food restaurants. Many are deciding that if that's all there is to lunch or supper— just food, minus any social sharing—they don't really need that hamburger. As a matter of fact, the time normally given to eating can be spent in other, more life-giving pursuits, such as exercise or reading or prayer.

THE WHAT, HOW, AND WHEN OF FASTING

Those whose religious obligations determine the nature and duration of their fast may want to skip this section. The following is written for those who are new to fasting or whose traditions allow them discretion to either partly or completely abstain from solids and liquids.

Right off the bat, I'm going to eliminate solids. I don't think simply cutting down on solid food merits the designation of fasting. Call it "reduced eating" or something like that, but not fasting. Words matter: When you say "I'm fasting," most people in the world will assume you are taking liquids at most.

The best way to begin in fasting is to ease into it. Start by giving up one meal, but do it with purpose and intention and frame it with prayer. Then, on the following week, drop two meals. The next time around, try a whole day. If your religious tradition allows the option of taking liquids, take them.

WHAT TO DRINK

Water and juice fasts are the two primary forms of fasts practiced. Water-only fasts tend to provide more of an intense fasting experience because the toxic release into the bloodstream is more concentrated and happens more quickly. If you've never fasted before, a juice and water fast is easier and the best way to begin. It enables you to maintain your accustomed daily energy level while continuing to work and exercise if you choose to do so. A juice fast will still help the body to detoxify and heal, though to a lesser extent. On the other hand, it will also keep the desire for food more alive through the taste of the juice, whereas in water fasting the desire for food passes more quickly. Both are good, but they are different. In longer fasts, those differences become more important than they are in a one-day fast.

Water, juices, herbal teas, and broth quiet the self, in all ways, so that it can hear and be more attentive to the Divine and focus more on this presence. Drinks like black coffee, nonherbal teas, and soft drinks stimulate the central nervous system at a time when we are trying to give the self a rest, a space and time for focusing on more internal realities. Artificially colored, flavored, and sweetened drinks recall the memory of food to the taste buds, arouse distracting hunger, and at the same time inhibit the purifying process that is going on in the digestive system.

When we drink only water, juices, or herbal teas during a fast, the body cleanses itself similarly to when we wring out a dirty sponge. The dirt in this case is the toxins and drugs that have been passing around in our circulatory system trying to become so thoroughly dissolved that they can pass through the fine structure of the body's "physiological sieve," the kidneys. These certain liquids are a faster's best friends since they facilitate the flushing-out of waste materials that keep us running at a low level, feeling sluggish and not much in the mood to give God joyful praise for the gift of life and health. Each of our two kidneys has a million efficient filters, and when the body is fasting, the kidneys step up their work of detoxification. All the energy that is not being used up in the laborious task of mastication, digestion, metabolism, and elimination is turned toward physical renewal.

Water fasting. Use bottled spring water at room temperature. Avoid tap water. Most tap water contains chlorine and fluorides, which are manufactured chemicals. If you're interested in cleansing your system, it doesn't makes sense to ingest more chemicals. In distilled water, many minerals and nutrients have been removed.

Apart from the oxygen in the air we breathe, the most important ingredient for humans is water, which constitutes between one-half and three-quarters of the weight of every human. This percentage is even higher in babies and young children than in adults, and in lean rather than obese individuals. The intracellular fluid—the water inside the individual cells—constitutes three-quarters of the total body water.

Although water generally is not thought of as a nutrient, it is essential to every bodily function. Every chemical change that occurs in the body takes place in the presence of water. In addition, water is the basis of every body fluid—blood, lymph, digestive juices, bile, perspiration, urine, and feces. It acts like oil in an engine, lubricating and preventing friction between moving parts, and it regulates body temperature through evaporation from the lungs and as the result of perspiration. The primary use of water in our bodies involves kidney function, since it is the kidneys through which waste products are excreted. Once this task is completed, water is made available within the body for other purposes.

Under normal circumstances, it is not very likely that an individual will ingest too much water. However, a person who is unusually thirsty or suddenly starts passing a great deal of urine should see a physician, since these may be symptoms of diabetes. Conversely, a swelling of parts of the body as a result of water retention also is a very strong indication of the need for medical attention. If you don't seem to be eliminating as much water as you're taking in and wonder where it's going, it's probably going right out through your pores in the most dynamic organ of the elimination network: your skin.

Juice fasting. In juice fasting, vitamins, minerals, enzymes, trace elements, and fresh raw vegetable juices are extremely beneficial in normalizing all body processes. They supply needed elements for the body's own healing activity and cell regeneration and expedite the recovery. These juices require no digestion and are easily assimilated directly into the bloodstream.

If you go this route, the juices should be as fresh as possible. In the best of all ideal worlds, juice organically grown fruits and vegetables at home right before drinking. The next best thing: Buy fresh raw juices at your local health-food store. A couple of caveats: Avoid juices that have pulp in them, and don't mix fruit and vegetable juices together (the mixture of the two may not sit well with your stomach). Dilute the sweeter juices such as orange, carrot, and apple by half with water to prevent shocking the finely balanced blood glucose system and its concomitant organ, the pancreas. The total juice or broth volume will generally be between 1.5 pints and 1.5 quarts per day, though some people may take up to a gallon of juices if they have been exercising strenuously. This juice volume is in addition to the recommended six to eight daily glasses of water, whether you are fasting or not.

SIDE EFFECTS YOU'RE LIKELY TO FEEL AND WHAT THEY MEAN

Eating has become such an important part of our lives that when we deprive ourselves of food and begin a fast, we may experience one or more mental and physical reactions: headaches, nausea, dizziness, gnawing in the stomach, dark urine, skin eruptions, excessive perspiration, coating on the tongue, bad breath, restless sleep, and elimination of mucus through the nose and mouth. These side effects have given fasting a bad name and made it unpopular. But if we realize these are signs of healing, we'll find that they're not so bad after all. As a matter of fact, they're blessings in disguise—steps on the way to feeling really well, both mentally and physically.

The good news is that they're transitory. They are indications that the body is ridding itself of waste materials. And the

best news is that some people won't experience the unpleasantness or discomforts at all, even though the purification is going
on. The faster's attitude has been known to make a big difference. People who approach the experience positively, acknowledging their apprehensions and fears but not allowing them to
hold sway, have the better record. But if you run into any of
those blessings in disguise, here's how to respond to them:

Gnawing in the stomach. It's not a genuine hunger pang (in
the sense that your body needs the food) or a distress signal. It's
just the alimentary tract accommodating itself to a reduced
workload. How to deal with it? Drink water more frequently—
a glass of water can satisfy what feels like a ravenous appetite.

Tiredness, nausea, headache, restless sleep. When you fast, the
waste in your body is loosened and sent into the circulation system to be discarded. When this is going on, you may feel lethargic. But once the waste is discarded, you begin to feel much
better. Nausea can be alleviated by drinking more water.
Headaches are often the result of caffeine withdrawal. Again,
drink more water. You may experience restlessness in sleep due
to increased dreaming (emotional detoxing!) or simply wake up
earlier than usual because on a fast day your body is already in a
resting mode.

Dizziness. Your blood pressure is lower when you fast, so
when you suddenly stand up after you've been sitting or lying
down, you may experience momentary dizziness. Sit first if
you've been lying down; and if you've been sitting, stand up next
to something you can hang on to for support.

HOW LONG TO FAST
This is basically a question to be answered through prayer.
Anything we do to deepen our awareness of God is done only at
the initiative of the Divine Spirit working in our hearts. It is God
who gives the idea, who inclines us to respond favorably to the
idea, and who urges us to move from idea to action. So the ques-

tion "How long should I fast?" is one to be resolved in the depths of your heart. Related considerations will be your situation in life, the particular "why" of a fast at this time, and the circumstances of your workload. There are certainly longer fasts than those envisioned by the religious ordinances at which we have looked, but they are outside the purview of this book. My intention here is simply to introduce you to, or reinvigorate you in, the moderate fasting practices proposed by your religious community or inspired by another religious community. If anyone wishes to go beyond that, there are many resources available to serve as a guide.

HOW TO COME OFF THE FAST

Gandhi once said that perhaps more caution and more restraint are necessary in breaking a fast than in keeping it. Breaking a fast is a very important and significant phase of the fasting process. The beneficial physiological effects can be quickly undone if the fast is incorrectly broken. In other words: Begin with little and take even that slowly. Eating too much too fast can lead to digestive upset and general disorder. Some things to keep in mind:

Pause for a prayer of thanksgiving before you begin to eat. Take your time with the meal. Give more attention than you normally do to color, taste, and texture. Eat slowly.

For a one-day fast, take one transitional meal. A transitional meal consists of natural foods void of overly processed ingredients such as white sugar, white flour, and preservatives. The meal should be designed to have a cleansing laxative effect, something along the lines of a raw vegetable salad with a base of grated carrots and grated cabbage to move like a big broom right through your intestines. Lemon juice makes a good dressing. Follow the salad with cooked vegetables, for instance, stewed tomatoes, spinach, squash, celery, or string beans. Or, the transitional meal could also be as simple as a piece of fruit or fresh vegetable soup with juice or herb tea. You'll find that a little bit of food can seem like a great sufficiency. Continue to drink lots of water.

The temptation to overeat is huge. Avoid turning around and overburdening your digestive system just after giving it a rest. Before you even come to the table or into the kitchen, be clear in your own mind what it is you want to eat and how much, then stick to it. Avoid eating meat, milk, cheese, butter, fish, nuts, and seeds right away. Eat lightly and just enough. Remember, it's a transitional meal back to your normal eating patterns, not the first normal meal. Allow the body that time to adjust from a detoxing program to an eating program.

WHEN TO FAST

In most of the religions we have looked at, there are days specifically designated as communal fast days: Yom Kippur and Tisha B'Av for Jews, Fridays in Lent for Catholics and Orthodox Christians, Ramadan for Muslims, the monthly fast Sunday for Mormons. And at the same time, each of these religions specifically states that individuals may fast at times of their own choosing throughout the year. When might it be appropriate to do so? From my own experience, I would suggest it can be undertaken with real benefit as an honest reaction to what's going on in your life. Perhaps these personal examples will make it clear:

My need for conversion. There are times when I know I need to turn again to God with renewed fervor. There are times when I know that I have failed morally, and I feel an inner desire to express my contrition and desire to begin anew. Times when deeper, more thorough self-examination and repentance are called for. Times when repeated petitionary prayer seems unavailing and direction is not forthcoming. Periods when I know that my prayer is distracted and half-hearted and falls back upon me as empty words. When I am too full of myself to really settle down and wait for God, when I'm in a mood to be distracted—to watch a movie or TV or visit friends—then it's time to fast. It's time to let God strip away what has piled up between us.

Fasting is one means of pulling ourselves up short before God and letting the penetrating gaze of the Holy One search our hearts. As soon as we begin to feel cluttered and out of touch, we can turn to God and ask to be shown why this coolness between us is happening. David's prayer can become our own:

> Search me, O God, and know my heart;
> test me, and know my thoughts.
> See if there is any wicked way in me,
> and lead me in the way everlasting.

> (Ps. 139:23, 24)

Why wait until we are backed against the wall and seeking God as the only alternative? God is concerned with our focus because it determines our steering, our direction. And periodically, depending on the constellation of circumstances in our lives, it needs readjustment. God allows us to get into certain situations that will show us whether our hearts are set upon God or intent upon pleasing ourselves. Is God central, or are things? What matters most to us?

Grief and distress. Another time in my life when I may turn to fasting as an honest reaction is in grief, distress, and mourning. A suicide bombing in Iraq that leaves fifty civilians dead in the market. Reports on the ongoing genocide in Sudan. A new outbreak of hostilities in Israel-Palestine. I can be standing at the bathroom mirror in the morning shaving or washing my face and the news coming over the radio suddenly freezes me, leaves me leaning on the sink, feeling beaten down with the seeming hopelessness and heaviness of all the distressing news, day after day.

After Paul had been knocked off his horse on the road to Damascus, he fasted for three days, waiting in total blindness for further instructions from the Lord. It must have been a time of complete upheaval and reversal of life purposes for him. His perplexity must have been extreme. In the Hebrew scriptures, Ezra was so disturbed by the sin of his countrymen that he found no better way to express the intensity of his grief and sorrow that this: "He did not eat bread or drink water, for he was mourning over the faithlessness of the exiles" (Ezra 10:6). David's fasting, too, was an honest reaction to the deaths of Saul and of Jonathan. He could not desire food while the emotions of shock and loss swept over him, so he set aside time for his reactions. He did not try to go on with business as usual, masking his feelings:

> Then David took hold of his clothes and tore them; and … mourned and wept, and fasted … for Saul, and for his son Jonathan, and for the army of the Lord and for the house of Israel, because they had fallen by the sword. (2 Sam. 1:11, 12)

In all these circumstances, fasting is a prayer of the whole person that comes from deep in the heart.

Fatigue. The recognition that I need a rest is another moment when fasting is an honest reaction. "Come to me, all you who are heavy burdened, and I will give you rest … learn of me and you will find rest for your souls" (Matt. 11:28). I am worn out. I am tired of the sound of my own voice. When someone comes to the door or the phone rings, it feels like an imposition. My mind keeps straying as I am listening to this person. Somebody calls a meeting and my first thought is, "How long will it last?" I don't even want to know what is in my heart because I don't have the energy to deal with it. I just saw my good friend, and it didn't feel special to me to see him at all. I feel driven. I can't laugh at the mess on my desk or in the house; I resent it.

These are cues to step back from it all. I need time to get in touch with myself and to pour out my heart to God. Rest is essential. Fasting makes it a total rest for *all* of me. In the Mosaic Law, a special day was set aside in which no work was to be done and the people were to fast. The reason? To free the people from daily cares and family responsibilities so that they could deal with their inner life. What a great idea!

Travel. The word *holiday* comes from the Old English word for "holy day." The word harks back to a time when rest time was holy time, a holy day. Oftentimes, unfortunately, when we come to that extended rest time in the year called "vacation" or "holiday," we plan, control, and package it so much that it's finished before it begins.

Sometimes going on a holiday in the spirit of a pilgrimage can provide a wonderful experience. A pilgrimage does not follow a laid-out plan or itinerary; it does not pursue a fixed aim or a limited purpose. It carries its meaning in itself, by relying on an inner urge that operates on two planes, physical and spiritual. It is a movement not only in the outer but equally in the inner space, a movement whose spontaneity is that of the nature of all life, that is, a movement that always starts from an invisible inner core.

When I approach my holiday in this spirit—whether it's just a day off or a three-week vacation—fasting often enters into it spontaneously. I may be driving from one place to another and just decide to keep right on going without stopping to eat; or perhaps the plane arrival and departure times are out of sync with mealtimes; or I may be trying to decide what food to take with me on a day hike or a bike ride, and the thought will come to me: "Why take anything at all?" If the time in front of me is planned out roughly rather than rigidly, if where I'm going and what I'll do amounts to no more than an expedient structure, a kind of loose net within which my sight will be on the little open spaces between the netting, tiny inspirations can suggest themselves along the way and find a fertile ground for response.

When time away is approached in the spirit of pilgrimage, one enters into it flexibly, waiting on God, expecting unforeseen paths to present themselves. And through all one sees and does and feels, there is a kind of alertness to the Divine Presence beneath the surface, an openness that is gently expectant, willing to be caught up and pulled into the freshness of divine play.

As crazy as it may sound, fasting can be like that: a secret shared between yourself and God, an act of a free spirit, a light-hearted feeling of liberation as you flout the conventions of eating and locate joy and interest elsewhere. The impulse to make a day in the middle of vacation a fast day, if responded to with the spirit of a pilgrim, can be a deeply enjoyable day that has a positive quality about it that is different from all the other days. And no wonder. It harks back to a time when a holiday was a holy time, a holy day.

The above examples are just some of the ways that fasting can serve us as a powerful way of praying from where we are. This is what spirituality today is asking us to do. To live with God-consciousness. To lift up our hearts and minds to God in all our circumstances. And God is not simply "out there," but in my body and spirit, in my neighbor, in my efforts to work for a just society, in my emotions and longings, in my struggle and joy, in my fasting and eating. As Gandhi said, "No matter from what motive you are fasting, during this precious time, think of your Maker, and of your relation to him and his other creation, and you will make discoveries you may not even have dreamed of."[7]

ALTERNATIVE FORMS OF FASTING

Fasting can relate to more than just food and drink. If your health or your age or your life circumstances—or those of anyone you know—do not permit fasting in the traditional sense, then make one or more of the following ways of fasting part of your life on a regular basis. And even for those who are able to fast from food and drink, these alternate forms can supplement a regular, traditional fast day or replace a day of fast.

Fast with Your Eyes

- Watch less TV and video; reflect more on your life through keeping a journal.
- Become informed about the causes of hunger in the world.

Fast with Your Ears

- Listen less to the radio, CDs, cassettes; listen more to your own inner heart and spirit.
- Be attentive to the words of others.
- Listen to and let yourself be challenged by the words expressed in the scriptures.

Fast with Your Mouth

- Take just one helping of the food that is served.
- Eat fewer sweets and processed foods, but appreciate more simple food and drink like water and good bread.

Fast with Your Hands

- Back off from things that agitate you.
- Take time to just sit and reflect, to rest and observe.
- Make time in your schedule to put your hands together in prayer.
- Share from your own goods with those who have less.

Fast with Your Feet

- Become more attuned to the modern compulsion to be always on the go; resist the impulse.
- Offer yourself a daily quiet half-hour of reading that nourishes your spirit.
- Learn quiet sitting in meditation.
- Make more time to welcome others to your home.

Fast with Your Body

- Attach less importance to external fashion and makeup.
- Reclaim your natural hair and skin color.
- When eating, practice stopping when you've had enough, rather than continuing to eat until you feel full.

Fast from Anger, Resentment, Bitterness

- Get to the bottom of why you're angry or resentful: What's the hidden demand underneath?
- Do the hard work of talking it through with the other, of expressing clearly what it is you are asking for.
- Pray for the grace of forgiving those who have hurt you.

Fast from Judging Others

- Unhook from conversations in which others are being disparaged, or contribute something positive to balance the negative things that are being said.
- Before making any judgments, recall how God looks compassionately on our faults.

Fast from Complaining

- When you're feeling inclined to complain, stop and look at all you are blessed with and give thanks instead.

Fast from the Presence of Your Children

- When you feel their absence, find some meaning in the emptiness and the silence.
- Choose life for them by supporting them graciously as they strike out to make their own marks in the world.
- Choose life for yourself by turning to and embracing new possibilities for living, growing, and loving.

Fast from Glossing Over Your Losses Too Quickly

- Allow yourself to feel the emptiness, the ache, the absence.

- Take the time to do the inner work of grieving.
- Resist the quick but superficial emotional fix, the easy fill-in.
- Risk listening in the silence to the soft voice of inner wisdom.

Fast from the Intimacy of a Spouse or Friend during a Temporary Absence

- Leave the heart space vacant and let your longing turn you toward God.
- Refresh your realization in the time of absence that relationship is life's blue-ribbon experience, that of this "food" we are meant to eat, and that without it we die.
- Let your desire for the presence of the other teach you that we were made for communion, and "our hearts are restless, Lord, until they rest in Thee."

Whatever form of fasting you choose, I would suggest you keep a journal. A good way to clarify your purpose or intention for the day is to put it in writing before you even begin. Record as well any thoughts and feelings that surface in the course of the day. The process of writing will draw you inward, oblige you to take time out of your normal routine for reflection. It will also provide you with a record of your experiences—your questions lived, fears harbored, insights gained, prayers answered, graces received. In the first chapter, I recounted leading a Bible study series entitled "The Adventure of Fasting" and how the title alone piqued people's curiosity. Fasting *is* an adventure—an adventure of the human spirit into uncharted waters, into a mysterious and faith-filled encounter with the divine mystery of God.

Fasting as a religious act increases our sensitivity to that mystery always and everywhere present to us. It is a passageway into the world of spirit to explore its territory and bring back a wisdom necessary for living a fulfilled life. It is an invitation to awareness, a call to compassion for the needy, a cry of distress and a song of joy. It is a discipline of self-restraint, a ritual of purification, and a sanctuary for offerings of atonement. It is a wellspring for the spiritually dry, a compass for the spiritually lost, and inner nourishment for the spiritually hungry.

In every culture and religion in history, fasting has been an instinctive and essential language in our communication with the Divine. Let us not be the ones who forget the reasons, the rituals, and the words.

NOTES

CHAPTER ONE

1. Thomas Ryan, *Fasting Rediscovered: A Guide to Health and Wholeness for Your Body-Spirit* (New York: Paulist Press, 1981).

CHAPTER TWO

1. Rabbi Jonathan Matt, "The Fast Days of *Tammuz* and *Av*," www.bridgesforpeace.com/publications/dispatch/biblicalfeasts/.
2. Arthur Green, *These Are the Words: A Vocabulary of Jewish Spiritual Life* (Woodstock, Vt.: Jewish Lights Publishing, 2002), 106, 107.
3. Aliza Bulow, "Connecting through Fasting," published on the Aish HaTorah website, www.aish.com/literacy/concepts/Connecting_Through_Fasting.asp. Reprinted with permission.

CHAPTER THREE

1. P. R. Régamy, *Redecouverte du Jeune* (Paris: Éditions du Cerf, 1959), 76, 127.
2. Ernest E. Larkin, "Asceticism," *The New Dictionary of Theology*, ed. Joseph Komonchak, Mary Collins, and Dermont A. Lane (Wilmington, Del.: Michael Glazier, 1987), 65.
3. Charles Cummings, *Monastic Practices* (Kalamazoo, Mich.: Cistercian Publications, 1986), 115, 118,119.
4. Ibid., 122, 126, 127.
5. Régamy, *Redecouverte du Jeune*, 124.
6. Ibid., 120.
7. *Baptism, Eucharist, and Ministry*, Faith and Order Paper no. 111 (Geneva: World Council of Churches, 1982), paragraphs 20–21.

8. For more information on the "fast from violence," see the website www.overcomingviolence.org or contact the U.S. Office of the World Council of Churches, 475 Riverside Drive, Room 915, New York, NY 10115, (212) 870-3533.
9. See the article on fasting at www.elca.org/prayer/resouces.html; *What Luther Says,* vol. 1 (St. Louis: Concordia Publishing House, 1959), 506.
10. U.S. National Conference of Catholic Bishops, "Pastoral Statement on Penance and Abstinence," November 18, 1966.
11. National Liturgical Office of the Canadian Conference of Catholic Bishops, "Living Lent" (leaflet), 1986.
12. Régamy, *Redecouverte du Jeune,* 136–149.
13. Larkin, "Asceticism," 66, 67.

CHAPTER FOUR

1. Thomas McElwain, "Islam in the Bible," www.submission.org/fasting-bible.html. This website calls itself the "best source for Islam (Submission) on the Internet" and offers many articles and resources.
2. Dr. Abu Ameenah Bilal Philips, "The Five Pillars of Islam: *Sawm,*" www.viewislam.com/pillars/pillar3.htm. The View Islam website was created for English-speaking non-Muslims interested in learning about Islam.
3. Afif A. Tabbarah, "The Spirit of Fasting in Islam," published on the SunniPath website, www.sunnipath.org, an Online Center for Traditional Islamic Knowledge.
4. Naseer Ahmad Faruqui Sahib, "Fasting in Islam," www.aaiil.org/text/articles/light/fastislm.shtml, hosted by the Lahore Amadiyya Movement for the Propagation of Islam.
5. Dr. Mansour Alam, "The Purpose of Fasting in Islam," www.icgt.org/monitor021112/fasting.htm, hosted by the Islamic Center of Greater Toledo.
6. S. A. Mawdudi, "The Meaning and Blessing of Fasting," www.islamicsociety.neu.edu/nonmuslims/fasting.pdf, hosted by the Islamic Society of Northeastern University.
7. Marmaduke Pickthall, "Holy Ramadan," www.playandlearn.org/ramadhan/r126.htm, a website providing informative articles on Islam.
8. Quoted in Pickthall, "Holy Ramadan."

9. Shahid Athar, MD, "Health Concerns for Believers: Contemporary Issues," www.islam-usa.com/h8.html.
10. "Ramadan: Rules and Regulations," comp. Ishaq Zahid, courtesy of the Islamic Information and News Network, vol. 4, no. 43.
11. Dr. Muhammad Hamidullah, "Why Fast?" posted on a personal website at www.angelfire.com/me/anneesa/whyfast.html.
12. Dr. Arafat El-Ashi, "Fasting in Islam," posted on a personal website at www.angelfire.com/me/anneesa/fastingislam.html.
13. Mawdudi, "The Meaning and Blessing of Fasting."
14. Ibid.
15. Philips, "The Five Pillars of Islam."

CHAPTER FIVE

1. This passage can be found in the *Mahabharata, Anusasana Parva,* Section CVI.
2. "Ekadasi," www.iskcon.com/basics/ekadasi.html, the International Society for Krishna Consciousness website.
3. The M. K. Gandhi Institute for Non-Violence was founded by Gandhi's grandson, Arun Gandhi. See www.gandhiinstitute.org. All the correspondence from which the excerpts here are drawn is available at this website.

CHAPTER SIX

1. A good popular telling of the story of the life of the Buddha is Thich Nhat Hanh, *Old Path, White Clouds: Walking in the Footsteps of the Buddha* (Boulder: Shambhala, 1982).

CHAPTER SEVEN

1. Joseph F. Smith, *Gospel Doctrine* (Salt Lake City: Deseret Book Co., 1939), 244.
2. Joseph B. Wirthlin, "The Law of the Fast," http://library.lds.org, published on the official website of the Church of Jesus Christ of Latter-day Saints.
3. Howard W. Hunter, "Fast Day," http://library.lds.org.
4. L. Tom Perry, "The Law of the Fast," http://library.lds.org.
5. B. H. Roberts, ed., *History of the Church of Jesus Christ of Latter-day Saints,* 3rd ed. (Salt Lake City: Deseret News, 1961), 7:413.
6. "Fast Offerings" in *Encyclopedia of Mormonism,* ed. Daniel H. Ludlow (New York: Macmillan, 1992), 2:501, 502.

7. Bruce R. McConkie, *Mormon Doctrine,* 2nd ed. (Salt Lake City: Bookcraft, 1966), 276.
8. Wirthlin, "The Law of the Fast."
9. Mary Jolley, "Fast and Testimony Meetings," *Encyclopedia of Mormonism,* 2:502.
10. Sheryl Condie Kempton, "Fasting: A Gift of Joy," *Ensign,* January 1978, 10. Reprinted with permission.

CHAPTER EIGHT

1. Bread for the World's website is www.bread.org. The organization can be reached at 50 F Street, NW, Suite 500, Washington, DC, 20001, 800-82-BREAD.
2. Al-Ghazzali, *The Mysteries of Fasting,* trans. Nabih Amin Faris (Lahore: Sh. Muhammad Ashraf, 1987), 41.

CHAPTER NINE

1. William C. Spohn, *Go and Do Likewise: Jesus and Ethics* (New York: Continuum, 1999), 38–40.
2. For those who may be interested in exploring longer fasts, the worldwide general list for retreat center fasting is found at www.retreatsonline.com/guide/fasting.htm.
3. Stephen Harrod Buhner, *The Fasting Path: The Way to Spiritual, Physical, and Emotional Enlightenment* (New York: Avery, 2003), 100.
4. Ibid., 92–94. Other works to consult are Margot Hellmiss and Norbert Kriegich, *Healthy Fasting* (New York: Sterling, 1999); Sidney MacDonald Baker, *Detoxification and Healing: The Key to Optimal Health* (New Canaan, Conn.: Keats, 1997); Alan Cott, MD, *Fasting: The Ultimate Diet* (Mamaroneck, N.Y.: Hastings House, 1997).
5. Buhner, *The Fasting Path,* 101.
6. See the Bread for the World website at www.bread.org/institute/obesity.html. However, as this site notes, research is emerging that suggests hunger, poverty, and obesity may be intricately linked. Recent work from Cornell University and the University of California at Davis suggest that obesity among poor women may be linked to their habit of periodically going without food so that their children can eat. Other factors also increase poor people's risk of obesity. Many low-income

Americans more likely are consuming foods low in nutritional quality and high in calories, fats, and sugars because these are the cheapest foods.

7. M. K. Gandhi, *Fasting in Satyagraha, Its Use and Abuse* (Ahmedabad, India: Navajivan, 1965), 76.

A C K N O W L E D G M E N T S

My heartfelt thanks

to Bernadette Latin and Jim Lucas who provided invaluable assistance with research;

to Debbie Rosenberg for advancing the work by keying in some of the material;

to Aliza Bulow, Rabbi Kerry M. Olitzky, Dr. Sheikh Ibrahim Negm, Swami Vasishta, Rev. Heng Sure, PhD, and Sheryl Condie Kempton, all of whom lent their own living voices in witness to the actual practice of fasting in their traditions;

to Jon Sweeney and SkyLight Paths Publishing for the invitation to write this book;

to project editor Sarah McBride, who conscientiously and with an even spirit kept production on stream and moving forward;

and to my editor, Maura Shaw, whose encouragement, suggestions, and editorial expertise have made positive and appreciated contributions all along the way.

Spirituality

Autumn: A Spiritual Biography of the Season
Edited by Gary Schmidt and Susan M. Felch; Illustrations by Mary Azarian

Autumn is a season of fruition and harvest, of thanksgiving and celebration of abundance and goodness of the earth. But it is also a season that starkly and realistically encourages us to see the limitations of our time. Warm and poignant pieces by Wendell Berry, David James Duncan, Robert Frost, A. Bartlett Giamatti, Kimiko Hahn, P. D. James, Julian of Norwich, Garret Keizer, Tracy Kidder, Anne Lamott, May Sarton, and many others rejoice in autumn as a time of preparation and reflection.   6 x 9, 320 pp, 5 b/w illus., HC, ISBN 1-59473-005-9 **$22.99**

Awakening the Spirit, Inspiring the Soul
30 Stories of Interspiritual Discovery in the Community of Faiths
Edited by Brother Wayne Teasdale and Martha Howard, MD; Foreword by Joan Borysenko, PhD

Thirty original spiritual mini-biographies that showcase the varied ways that people come to faith—and what that means—in today's multi-religious world.
6 x 9, 224 pp, HC, ISBN 1-59473-039-3 **$21.99**

Winter: A Spiritual Biography of the Season
Edited by Gary Schmidt and Susan M. Felch; Illustrations by Barry Moser

Delves into the varied feelings that winter conjures in us, calling up both the barrenness and the beauty of the natural world in wintertime. Includes selections by Will Campbell, Rachel Carson, Annie Dillard, Donald Hall, Ron Hansen, Jane Kenyon, Jamaica Kincaid, Barry Lopez, Kathleen Norris, John Updike, E. B. White, and many others. "This outstanding anthology features top-flight nature and spirituality writers on the fierce, inexorable season of winter.... Remarkably lively and warm, despite the icy subject." —*Publishers Weekly* Starred Review

6 x 9, 288 pp, 6 b/w illus., Deluxe PB w/flaps, ISBN 1-893361-92-6 **$18.95**; HC, ISBN 1-893361-53-5 **$21.95**

The Alphabet of Paradise: An A–Z of Spirituality for Everyday Life
by Howard Cooper 5 x 7¾, 224 pp, Quality PB, ISBN 1-893361-80-2 **$16.95**

Creating a Spiritual Retirement: A Guide to the Unseen Possibilities in Our Lives
by Molly Srode 6 x 9, 208 pp, b/w photos, Quality PB, ISBN 1-59473-050-42 **$14.99**; HC, ISBN 1-893361-75-6 **$19.95**

The Geography of Faith: Underground Conversations on Religious, Political and Social Change   *by Daniel Berrigan and Robert Coles; Updated introduction and afterword by the authors*   6 x 9, 224 pp, Quality PB, ISBN 1-893361-40-3 **$16.95**

God Lives in Glass: Reflections of God for Adults through the Eyes of Children
by Robert J. Landy, PhD; Foreword by Sandy Eisenberg Sasso
7 x 6, 64 pp, HC, Full-color illus., ISBN 1-893361-30-6 **$12.95**

God Within: Our Spiritual Future—As Told by Today's New Adults   *Edited by Jon M. Sweeney and the Editors at SkyLight Paths* 6 x 9, 176 pp, Quality PB, ISBN 1-893361-15-2 **$14.95**

Jewish Spirituality: A Brief Introduction for Christians   *by Lawrence Kushner*
5½ x 8½, 112 pp, Quality PB, ISBN 1-58023-150-0 **$12.95** *(a Jewish Lights book)*

A Jewish Understanding of the New Testament
by Rabbi Samuel Sandmel; New preface by Rabbi David Sandmel
5½ x 8½, 384 pp, Quality PB, ISBN 1-59473-048-2 **$19.99**

Journeys of Simplicity: Traveling Light with Thomas Merton, Basho, Edward Abbey, Annie Dillard & Others   *by Philip Harnden* 5 x 7¼, 128 pp, HC, ISBN 1-893361-76-4 **$16.95**

Keeping Spiritual Balance As We Grow Older: More than 65 Creative Ways to Use Purpose, Prayer, and the Power of Spirit to Build a Meaningful Retirement
by Molly and Bernie Srode 8 x 8, 224 pp, Quality PB, ISBN 1-59473-042-3 **$16.99**

The Monks of Mount Athos: A Western Monk's Extraordinary Spiritual Journey on Eastern Holy Ground   *by M. Basil Pennington, ocso; Foreword by Archimandrite Dionysios*
6 x 9, 256 pp, 10+ b/w line drawings, Quality PB, ISBN 1-893361-78-0 **$18.95**

One God Clapping: The Spiritual Path of a Zen Rabbi   *by Alan Lew with Sherrill Jaffe*
5½ x 8½, 336 pp, Quality PB, ISBN 1-58023-115-2 **$16.95** *(a Jewish Lights book)*

Sacred Texts—SkyLight Illuminations Series
Andrew Harvey, series editor

Offers today's spiritual seeker an enjoyable entry into the great classic texts of the world's spiritual traditions. Each classic is presented in an accessible translation, with facing pages of guided commentary from experts, giving you the keys you need to understand the history, context, and meaning of the text. This series enables readers of all backgrounds to experience and understand classic spiritual texts directly, and to make them a part of their lives. Andrew Harvey writes the foreword to each volume, an insightful, personal introduction to each classic.

Bhagavad Gita
Annotated & Explained
Translation by Shri Purohit Swami; Annotation by Kendra Crossen Burroughs
"The very best Gita for first-time readers." —Ken Wilber. Millions of people turn daily to India's most beloved holy book, whose universal appeal has made it popular with non-Hindus and Hindus alike. This edition introduces you to the characters, explains references and philosophical terms, shares the interpretations of famous spiritual leaders and scholars, and more.
5½ x 8½, 192 pp, Quality PB, ISBN 1-893361-28-4 **$16.95**

Dhammapada
Annotated & Explained
Translation by Max Müller and revised by Jack Maguire; Annotation by Jack Maguire
The Dhammapada—believed to have been spoken by the Buddha himself over 2,500 years ago—contain most of Buddhism's central teachings. This timeless text concisely and inspirationally portrays the route a person travels as he or she advances toward enlightenment and describes the fundamental role of mental conditioning in making us who we are.
5½ x 8½, 160 pp, b/w photographs, Quality PB, ISBN 1-893361-42-X **$14.95**

The Gospel of Thomas
Annotated & Explained
Translation and annotation by Stevan Davies
Discovered in 1945, this collection of aphoristic sayings sheds new light on the origins of Christianity and the intriguing figure of Jesus, portraying the Kingdom of God as a present fact about the world, rather than a future promise or future threat.
5½ x 8½, 192 pp, Quality PB, ISBN 1-893361-45-4 **$16.95**

Hasidic Tales
Annotated & Explained
Translation and annotation by Rabbi Rami Shapiro
Introduces the legendary tales of the impassioned Hasidic rabbis, which demonstrate the spiritual power of unabashed joy, offer lessons for leading a holy life, and remind us that the Divine can be found in the everyday.
5½ x 8½, 240 pp, Quality PB, ISBN 1-893361-86-1 **$16.95**

The Hebrew Prophets
Selections Annotated & Explained
Translation and annotation by Rabbi Rami Shapiro
Focuses on the central themes covered by all the Hebrew prophets: moving from ignorance to wisdom, injustice to justice, cruelty to compassion, and despair to joy, and challenges us to engage in justice, kindness, and humility in every aspect of our lives.
5½ x 8½, 224 pp, Quality PB, ISBN 1-59473-037-7 **$16.99**

Sacred Texts—SkyLight Illuminations Series
Andrew Harvey, series editor

The Hidden Gospel of Matthew: Annotated & Explained
Translation and annotation by Ron Miller
Takes you deep into the text cherished around the world to discover the words and events that have the strongest connection to the historical Jesus. Reveals the underlying story of Matthew, a story that transcends the traditional theme of an atoning death and focuses instead on Jesus's radical call for personal transformation and social change.
5½ x 8½, 272 pp, Quality PB, ISBN 1-59473-038-5 **$16.99**

The Secret Book of John
The Gnostic Gospel—Annotated & Explained
Translation and annotation by Stevan Davies
Introduces the most significant and influential text of the ancient Gnostic religion. This central myth of Gnosticism tells the story of how God fell from perfect Oneness to imprisonment in the material world, and how by knowing our divine nature and our divine origins—that we are one with God—we reverse God's descent and find our salvation.
5½ x 8½, 208 pp, Quality PB, ISBN 1-59473-082-2 **$16.99**

Rumi and Islam: Selections from His Stories, Poems, and Discourses—Annotated & Explained
Translation and annotation by Ibrahim Gamard
Offers a new way of thinking about Rumi's poetry. Focuses on Rumi's place within the Sufi tradition of Islam, providing insight into the mystical side of the religion—one that has love of God at its core and sublime wisdom teachings as its pathways.
5½ x 8½, 240 pp, Quality PB, ISBN 1-59473-002-4 **$15.99**

Selections from the Gospel of Sri Ramakrishna
Annotated & Explained
Translation by Swami Nikhilananda; Annotation by Kendra Crossen Burroughs
The words of India's greatest example of God-consciousness and mystical ecstasy in recent history. Introduces the fascinating world of the Indian mystic and the universal appeal of his message that has inspired millions of devotees for more than a century.
5½ x 8½, 240 pp, b/w photographs, Quality PB, ISBN 1-893361-46-2 **$16.95**

The Way of a Pilgrim: Annotated & Explained
Translation and annotation by Gleb Pokrovsky
This classic of Russian spirituality is the delightful account of one man who sets out to learn the prayer of the heart—also known as the "Jesus prayer"—and how the practice transforms his life.
5½ x 8½, 160 pp, Illus., Quality PB, ISBN 1-893361-31-4 **$14.95**

Zohar: Annotated & Explained
Translation and annotation by Daniel C. Matt
The best-selling author of *The Essential Kabbalah* brings together in one place the most important teachings of the Zohar, the canonical text of Jewish mystical tradition. Guides you step by step through the midrash, mystical fantasy, and Hebrew scripture that make up the Zohar, explaining the inner meanings in facing-page commentary.
5½ x 8½, 176 pp, Quality PB, ISBN 1-893361-51-9 **$15.99**

Children's Spiritual Biography

MULTICULTURAL, NONDENOMINATIONAL, NONSECTARIAN

Ten Amazing People
And How They Changed the World
by Maura D. Shaw; Foreword by Dr. Robert Coles
Full-color illus. by Stephen Marchesi

For ages 7 & up

Black Elk • Dorothy Day • Malcolm X • Mahatma Gandhi • Martin Luther King, Jr. • Mother Teresa • Janusz Korczak • Desmond Tutu • Thich Nhat Hanh • Albert Schweitzer

This vivid, inspirational, and authoritative book will open new possibilities for children by telling the stories of how ten of the past century's greatest leaders changed the world in important ways.

8½ x 11, 48 pp, HC, Full-color illus., ISBN 1-893361-47-0 **$17.95** *For ages 7 & up*

Spiritual Biographies for Young People—For ages 7 and up

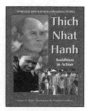 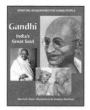 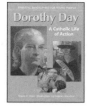 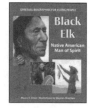

Black Elk: Native American Man of Spirit
by Maura D. Shaw; Full-color illus. by Stephen Marchesi
Through historically accurate illustrations and photos, inspiring age-appropriate activities, and Black Elk's own words, this colorful biography introduces children to a remarkable person who ensured that the traditions and beliefs of his people would not be forgotten.
6¾ x 8¾, 32 pp, HC, Full-color illus., ISBN 1-59473-043-1 **$12.99**

Dorothy Day: A Catholic Life of Action
by Maura D. Shaw; Full-color illus. by Stephen Marchesi
Introduces children to one of the most inspiring women of the twentieth century, a down-to-earth spiritual leader who saw the presence of God in every person she met. Includes practical activities, a timeline, and a list of important words to know.
6¾ x 8¾, 32 pp, HC, Full-color illus., ISBN 1-59473-011-3 **$12.99**

Gandhi: India's Great Soul
by Maura D. Shaw; Full-color illus. by Stephen Marchesi
There are a number of biographies of Gandhi written for young readers, but this is the only one that balances a simple text with illustrations, photographs, and activities that encourage children and adults to talk about how to make changes happen without violence. Introduces children to important concepts of freedom, equality, and justice among people of all backgrounds and religions.
6¾ x 8¾, 32 pp, HC, Full-color illus., ISBN 1-893361-91-8 **$12.95**

Thich Nhat Hanh: Buddhism in Action
by Maura D. Shaw; Full-color illus. by Stephen Marchesi
Warm illustrations, photos, age-appropriate activities, and Thich Nhat Hanh's own poems introduce a great man to children in a way they can understand and enjoy. Includes a list of important Buddhist words to know.
6¾ x 8¾, 32 pp, HC, Full-color illus., ISBN 1-893361-87-X **$12.95**

Global Spiritual Perspectives

Spiritual Perspectives on America's Role as Superpower

by the Editors at SkyLight Paths

Are we the world's good neighbor or a global bully? From a spiritual perspective, explores broader issues surrounding the use of American power around the world, including in Iraq and the Middle East.Contributors:

Dr. Beatrice Bruteau • Rev. Dr. Joan Brown Campbell • Tony Campolo • Rev. Forrest Church • Lama Surya Das • Matthew Fox • Kabir Helminski • Thich Nhat Hanh • Eboo Patel • Abbot M. Basil Pennington, ocso • Dennis Prager • Rosemary Radford Ruether • Wayne Teasdale • Rev. William McD.Tully • Rabbi Arthur Waskow • John Wilson

5½ x 8½, 256 pp, Quality PB, ISBN 1-893361-81-0 **$16.95**

Spiritual Perspectives on Globalization, 2nd Edition

Making Sense of Economic and Cultural Upheaval

by Ira Rifkin; Foreword by Dr. David Little, Harvard Divinity School

What is globalization? What are spiritually minded people saying and doing about it? This edition includes a new Afterword and Discussion Guide designed for group use.

5½ x 8½, 256 pp, Quality PB, ISBN 1-59473-045-8 **$16.99**

Meditation / Prayer

Prayers to an Evolutionary God

by William Cleary; Afterword by Diarmuid O'Murchu

Inspired by the spiritual and scientific teachings of Diarmuid O'Murchu and Teilhard de Chardin, Cleary reveals that religion and science can be combined to create an expanding view of the universe and God—an evolutionary faith.

6 x 9, 208 pp, HC, ISBN 1-59473-006-7 **$21.99**

The Song of Songs: A Spiritual Commentary

by M. Basil Pennington, ocso; Illustrations by Phillip Ratner

Join M. Basil Pennington as he ruminates on the Bible's most challenging mystical text. You will follow a path into the Songs that weaves through his inspired words and the evocative drawings of Jewish artist Phillip Ratner.

6 x 9, 160 pp, HC, 14 b/w illus., ISBN 1-59473-004-0 **$19.99**

Women of Color Pray: Voices of Strength, Faith, Healing, Hope, and Courage   Edited and with Introductions by Christal M. Jackson

Through these prayers, poetry, lyrics, meditations and affirmations, you will share in the strong and undeniable connection women of color share with God. It will challenge you to explore new ways of prayerful expression.

5 x 7¼, 240 pp, Quality PB, ISBN 1-59473-077-6 **$15.99**

The Art of Public Prayer, 2nd Edition: Not for Clergy Only

by Lawrence A. Hoffman   6 x 9, 288 pp, Quality PB, ISBN 1-893361-06-3 **$18.95**

Finding Grace at the Center: The Beginning of Centering Prayer

by M. Basil Pennington, ocso, Thomas Keating, ocso, and Thomas E. Clarke, sj

5 x 7¼, 112 pp, HC, ISBN 1-893361-69-1 **$14.95**

A Heart of Stillness: A Complete Guide to Learning the Art of Meditation

by David A. Cooper   5½ x 8½, 272 pp, Quality PB, ISBN 1-893361-03-9 **$16.95**

Meditation without Gurus: A Guide to the Heart of Practice

by Clark Strand   5½ x 8½, 192 pp, Quality PB, ISBN 1-893361-93-4 **$16.95**

Praying with Our Hands: Twenty-One Practices of Embodied Prayer from the World's Spiritual Traditions   by Jon M. Sweeney; Photographs by Jennifer J. Wilson; Foreword by Mother Tessa Bielecki; Afterword by Taitetsu Unno, PhD

8 x 8, 96 pp, 22 duotone photographs, Quality PB, ISBN 1-893361-16-0 **$16.95**

Silence, Simplicity & Solitude: A Complete Guide to Spiritual Retreat at Home

by David A. Cooper   5½ x 8½, 336 pp, Quality PB, ISBN 1-893361-04-7 **$16.95**

Three Gates to Meditation Practice: A Personal Journey into Sufism, Buddhism, and Judaism   by David A. Cooper   5½ x 8½, 240 pp, Quality PB, ISBN 1-893361-22-5 **$16.95**

Women Pray: Voices through the Ages, from Many Faiths, Cultures, and Traditions

Edited and with introductions by Monica Furlong

5 x 7¼, 256 pp, Quality PB, ISBN 1-59473-071-7 **$15.99**;

Deluxe HC with ribbon marker, ISBN 1-893361-25-X **$19.95**

Spirituality

Prayer for People Who Think Too Much
A Guide to Everyday, Anywhere Prayer from the World's Faith Traditions   *by Mitch Finley*
5½ x 8½, 224 pp, Quality PB, ISBN 1-893361-21-7 **$16.95**; HC, ISBN 1-893361-00-4 **$21.95**

The Shaman's Quest: Journeys in an Ancient Spiritual Practice
by Nevill Drury; with a Basic Introduction to Shamanism by Tom Cowan
5½ x 8½, 208 pp, Quality PB, ISBN 1-893361-68-3 **$16.95**

Show Me Your Way: The Complete Guide to Exploring Interfaith Spiritual Direction
by Howard A. Addison   5½ x 8½, 240 pp, Quality PB, ISBN 1-893361-41-1 **$16.95**;
HC, ISBN 1-893361-12-8 **$21.95**

Spirituality 101: The Indispensable Guide to Keeping—or Finding—Your Spiritual Life
on Campus   *by Harriet L Schwartz, with contributions from college students at nearly thirty campuses across the United States*   6 x 9, 272 pp, Quality PB, ISBN 1-59473-000-8 **$16.99**

Spiritually Incorrect: Finding God in All the Wrong Places
by Dan Wakefield; Illus. by Marian DelVecchio
5½ x 8½, 192 pp, b/w illus., HC, ISBN 1-893361-88-8 **$21.95**

Spiritual Manifestos: Visions for Renewed Religious Life in America from Young
Spiritual Leaders of Many Faiths   *Edited by Niles Elliot Goldstein; Preface by Martin E. Marty*
6 x 9, 256 pp, HC, ISBN 1-893361-09-8 **$21.95**

A Walk with Four Spiritual Guides: Krishna, Buddha, Jesus, and Ramakrishna
by Andrew Harvey   5½ x 8½, 192 pp, 10 b/w photos & illus., HC, ISBN 1-893361-73-X **$21.95**

What Matters: Spiritual Nourishment for Head and Heart
by Frederick Franck   5 x 7¼, 144 pp, 50+ b/w illus., HC, ISBN 1-59473-013-X **$16.99**

Who Is My God?, 2nd Edition
An Innovative Guide to Finding Your Spiritual Identity
Created by the Editors at SkyLight Paths   6 x 9, 160 pp, Quality PB, ISBN 1-59473-014-8 **$15.99**

Spirituality—A Week Inside

Come and Sit: A Week Inside Meditation Centers
by Marcia Z. Nelson; Foreword by Wayne Teasdale
The insider's guide to meditation in a variety of different spiritual traditions. Traveling through Buddhist, Hindu, Christian, Jewish, and Sufi traditions, this essential guide takes you to different meditation centers to meet the teachers and students and learn about the practices, demystifying the meditation experience.
6 x 9, 224 pp, b/w photographs, Quality PB, ISBN 1-893361-35-7 **$16.95**

Lighting the Lamp of Wisdom: A Week Inside a Yoga Ashram
by John Ittner; Foreword by Dr. David Frawley
This insider's guide to Hindu spiritual life takes you into a typical week of retreat inside a yoga ashram to demystify the experience and show you what to expect from your own visit. Includes a discussion of worship services, meditation and yoga classes, chanting and music, work practice, and more.   6 x 9, 192 pp, b/w photographs, Quality PB, ISBN 1-893361-52-7 **$15.95**; HC, ISBN 1-893361-37-3 **$24.95**

Making a Heart for God: A Week Inside a Catholic Monastery
by Dianne Aprile; Foreword by Brother Patrick Hart, ocso
This essential guide to experiencing life in a Catholic monastery takes you to the Abbey of Gethsemani—the Trappist monastery in Kentucky that was home to author Thomas Merton—to explore the details. "More balanced and informative than the popular *The Cloister Walk* by Kathleen Norris." —*Choice: Current Reviews for Academic Libraries*   6 x 9, 224 pp, b/w photographs, Quality PB, ISBN 1-893361-49-7 **$16.95**; HC, ISBN 1-893361-14-4 **$21.95**

Waking Up: A Week Inside a Zen Monastery
by Jack Maguire; Foreword by John Daido Loori, Roshi
An essential guide to what it's like to spend a week inside a Zen Buddhist monastery.   6 x 9, 224 pp, b/w photographs, Quality PB, ISBN 1-893361-55-1 **$16.95**; HC, ISBN 1-893361-13-6 **$21.95**

Spiritual Practice

Divining the Body
Reclaim the Holiness of Your Physical Self   *by Jan Phillips*
A practical and inspiring guidebook for connecting the body and soul in spiritual practice. Leads you into a milieu of reverence, mystery, and delight, helping you discover a redeemed sense of self.
8 x 8, 256 pp, Quality PB, ISBN 1-59473-080-6 **$16.99**

Finding Time for the Timeless
Spirituality in the Workweek   *by John McQuiston II*
Simple, refreshing stories that provide you with examples of how you can refocus and enrich your daily life using prayer or meditation, ritual, and other forms of spiritual practice.   5½ x 6½, 208 pp, HC, ISBN 1-59473-035-0 **$17.99**

The Gospel of Thomas: A Guidebook for Spiritual Practice
by Ron Miller; Translations by Stevan Davies
An innovative guide to bring a new spiritual classic into daily life. Offers a way to translate the wisdom of the Gospel of Thomas into daily practice, manifesting in your life the same consciousness revealed in Jesus of Nazareth. Written for readers of all religious backgrounds, this guidebook will help you to apply Jesus's wisdom to your own life and to the world around you.
6 x 9, 160 pp, Quality PB, ISBN 1-59473-047-4 **$14.99**

The Knitting Way: A Guide to Spiritual Self-Discovery
by Linda Skolnik and Janice MacDaniels
Through sharing stories, hands-on explorations, and daily cultivation, Skolnik and MacDaniels help you see beyond the surface of a simple craft in order to discover ways in which nuances of knitting can apply to the larger scheme of life and spirituality. Includes original knitting patterns.
7 x 9, 192 pp, Quality PB, ISBN 1-59473-079-2 **$16.99**

Earth, Water, Fire, and Air: Essential Ways of Connecting to Spirit
by Cait Johnson   6 x 9, 224 pp, HC, ISBN 1-893361-65-9 **$19.95**

Forty Days to Begin a Spiritual Life
Today's Most Inspiring Teachers Help You on Your Way
Edited by Maura Shaw and the Editors at SkyLight Paths; Foreword by Dan Wakefield
7 x 9, 144 pp, Quality PB, ISBN 1-893361-48-9 **$16.95**

Labyrinths from the Outside In
Walking to Spiritual Insight—A Beginner's Guide
by Donna Schaper and Carole Ann Camp
6 x 9, 208 pp, b/w illus. and photographs, Quality PB, ISBN 1-893361-18-7 **$16.95**

Practicing the Sacred Art of Listening: A Guide to Enrich Your Relationships and Kindle Your Spiritual Life—The Listening Center Workshop
by Kay Lindahl   8 x 8, 176 pp, Quality PB, ISBN 1-893361-85-3 **$16.95**

The Sacred Art of Bowing: Preparing to Practice
by Andi Young   5½ x 8½, 128 pp, b/w illus., Quality PB, ISBN 1-893361-82-9 **$14.95**

The Sacred Art of Chant: Preparing to Practice
by Ana Hernandez   5½ x 8½, 192 pp, Quality PB, ISBN 1-59473-036-9 **$15.99**

The Sacred Art of Fasting: Preparing to Practice
by Thomas Ryan, CSP   5½ x 8½, 176 pp, Quality PB, ISBN 1-59473-078-4 **$15.99**

The Sacred Art of Listening: Forty Reflections for Cultivating a Spiritual Practice
by Kay Lindahl; Illustrations by Amy Schnapper
8 x 8, 160 pp, Illus., Quality PB, ISBN 1-893361-44-6 **$16.99**

Sacred Speech: A Practical Guide for Keeping Spirit in Your Speech
by Rev. Donna Schaper   6 x 9, 176 pp, Quality PB, ISBN 1-59473-068-7 **$15.99**;
HC, ISBN 1-893361-74-8 **$21.95**

AVAILABL[...] OKSTORES.
TRY YOUR BOOKSTORE FIRST.

Spiritual Poetry—The Mystic Poets

Experience these mystic poets as you never have before. Each beautiful, compact book includes: A brief introduction to the poet's time and place; a summary of the major themes of the poet's mysticism and religious tradition; essential selections from the poet's most important works; and an appreciative preface by a contemporary spiritual writer.

 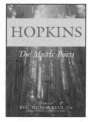  

Hafiz: The Mystic Poets
Preface by Ibrahim Gamard
Hafiz is known throughout the world as Persia's greatest poet, with sales of his poems in Iran today only surpassed by those of the Qur'an itself. His probing and joyful verse speaks to people from all backgrounds who long to taste and feel divine love and experience harmony with all living things.
5 x 7¼, 144 pp. [...]

Hopkin[s]
Preface by [...]
Gerard [...] [...]anguage and
startling [...] [...]vely, beneath
the surfa[...]
5 x 7¼, 112[...]

Tagor[e]
Preface b[...]
Rabind[...] [...] great mystic, Tag[...] [...]ert Einstein
and Ma[...] [...]utiful sampling of[...] [...]s a glimpse
into his[...]
5 x 7¼, 14[...]

Whitm[an]
Preface b[...]
Walt Wh[...] [...]ntury. This
beautifu[...] [...]d selections
from his[...] [...]l themes—
love for[...]
5 x 7¼, 19[...]

Or[...] [...]ishing
Sunset[...] [...]nt 05091
Tel[...] [...]s.com
Credit card orders: (800) 962-4544 (8:30AM–5:30PM ET Monday–Friday)
Generous discounts on quantity orders. SATISFACTION GUARANTEED. Prices subject to change.